Also by Barbara Robinette Moss

Change Me into Zeus's Daughter

Fierce

A MEMOIR

Barbara Robinette Moss

SCRIBNER
New York   London   Toronto   Sydney

SCRIBNER
1230 Avenue of the Americas
New York, NY 10020

SCRIBNER and design are trademarks of Macmillan Library Reference USA, Inc.,
used under license by Simon & Schuster, the publisher of this work.

For information about special discounts for bulk purchases,
please contact Simon & Schuster Special Sales:
1-800-456-6798 or business@simonandschuster.com

DESIGNED BY ERICH HOBBING

Text set in Adobe Caslon

Manufactured in the United States of America

1 3 5 7 9 10 8 6 4 2

Library of Congress Cataloging-in-Publication Data

Moss, Barbara Robinette.
Fierce: a memoir/Barbara Robinette Moss.
p. cm.
1. Moss, Barbara Robinette. 2. Adult children of alcoholics—United States—Biography.
I. Title.
HV5132.M673 2004
362.292'4'092—dc22
[B]
2004048188

ISBN 0-7432-2945-2

This book is dedicated to
Rosemary James and *Joseph DeSalvo*,
founders of The Pirate's Alley Faulkner Society, New Orleans, Louisiana,
and to *Jack Davis*,
the 1996 Personal Essay judge for The William Faulkner Creative
Writing Competition, sponsored by The Pirate's Alley Faulkner Society.
These three wonderful people
lovingly launched my writing career.

Love After Love

The time will come
when, with elation,
you will greet yourself arriving
at your own door, in your own mirror,
and each with a smile at the other's welcome,

and say, sit here. Eat
You will love again the stranger who was yourself.
Give wine. Give bread. Give back your heart
to itself, to the stranger who has loved you
all your life, whom you ignored
for another, who knows you by heart.
Take down the love letters from the bookshelf,

the photographs, the desperate notes,
peel your own image from the mirror.
Sit. Feast on your life.

DEREK WALCOTT

Contents

Foreword

When I was a girl, my mother made patchwork quilts for our beds. Raising eight children, she didn't have time for the elaborate designs her own mother had made: Dresden plate, bear paw, Martha Washington star. Mother's quilts were sewn together in a hurry, swatches of dark tweed, houndstooth, and corduroy, cut from old hand-me-down coats, the design brightened with shocks of red and yellow. I'd watch her work, taking a square of black wool from one stack, a rectangle of pale blue from another, her pattern created seemingly haphazardly as she worked. Yet the finished quilts were bold and complex, each piece of colored fabric relying on the one next to it for strength and support.

Fierce was written like one of my mother's quilts. The chapters, like seemingly separate pieces of cloth sewn together, create a pattern, the very thread of this life.

For those who have lived similar circumstances, and for those who haven't but want to better understand their friends and loved ones who have—I hope you will find warmth, and ultimately comfort, in these words.

PROLOGUE

Birmingham, Alabama, 1965

magic

Our neighbor asked my brother Willie, and my sister Doris Ann, and me to pull the weeds from his sidewalk. When we finished, he paid us a nickel apiece, and we headed down to 50th Street Delicatessen to buy candy.

A little bell jingled as we entered the store, and Sylvester, the owner, came from behind the meat counter, wiping his hands on his apron, and stood behind the cash register, which sat on the penny candy counter. The penny candy counter had everything: caramels, sour balls, apple grasshoppers, wax Coca-Cola bottles, candy cigarettes, banana bikes, licorice whips, and more.

Without hesitation, Doris Ann snatched up two cherry jaw-breakers. Willie nudged me and asked, "What are you going to buy, Barbara?"

I studied the bins of brightly wrapped candies. My favorites were the caramel squares, but they'd be gone in a minute. *Something that will last,* I pondered.

"Here's what you're looking for," Sylvester said, pointing to a shallow box next to the cash register. We peered into the box. Two dozen little round balls jumped rhythmically.

"Mexican jumping beans," he said. "They're magic." He waited a moment for that bit of information to sink in, then, waving his hand over the box, he said, "Go ahead. Pick one up."

Wide-eyed, Willie lifted a bean from the box and placed it in his palm. At first it didn't move and we stuck our faces closer. It jumped, and so did we.

"Wow," we said simultaneously.

Willie held the bean between his thumb and index finger. "This is a real Mexican jumping bean?"

Sylvester chuckled. "The real thing. For a penny, you get your wish."

Willie and I quickly dug our nickels from our pockets and slapped them on the counter. We watched to see which beans jumped with the most zeal and carefully lifted them from the box into our palms.

Doris Ann was reluctant to put her jawbreakers back. Finally she said, "I'm just going to buy three. I've only got three wishes anyway." She handed over her nickel and picked out three jumping beans. We headed out the door, lost in our dreams.

"Don't blow all your wishes on candy," Sylvester shouted. We ignored him.

As the beans continued to wiggle in my palm, I decided the fate of each wish. *This one is for a horse, because—well, because I need a horse.* I thought about our overgrown backyard, wondering whether horses liked to eat dandelions and kudzu. *They like oats; it makes their coats shiny.* I had checked out all the books from the Anna Stuart Dupuy School library on how to groom a horse.

This one is for ice skates. I had also checked out books on ice-skating ("The life story of Carol Heiss") because I wanted to be an ice-skater, a real dilemma since it never got cold enough in Alabama for the local ponds and waterways to freeze.

Number three: Zap me in front of The Last Supper *so I can see it for real.* Dad wouldn't let us plug in his light-up picture of *The Last Supper.* He was afraid we'd break his *investment.* "A one-of-a-kind," he called it, convinced that it would be worth a lot of money someday. I wanted to see the real one, the big one, the one Leonardo da Vinci had painted.

As I walked down the sidewalk, I slipped into my favorite daydream of becoming a famous artist. Suddenly, *I* had painted *The Last Supper.* I tumbled along in that fog for a minute, then snapped out of it and got back to the task at hand.

Number four: Make Dad quit drinking and quit yelling at everybody.
I thought about the night before. Dad had come home from the bar
at 3 A.M. and gotten everybody out of bed to clean up the house and
cut the grass. The police came and made my brother Stewart shut off
the lawn mower. After they left, Dad yelled at Mother for not making Stewart cut the grass earlier that day.

I studied the last bean and decided I'd give it to Mother so she
could wish for whatever she wanted.

Suddenly Willie took off running. "Stewart!" he shouted. "Stewart!" Doris Ann and I ran after him, careful not to drop our beans.

Stewart stood in front of the house with his paper-route canvas
bag stuffed with the *Birmingham News* hanging over his shoulder.
Breathless, we surrounded him.

"Look," Willie said, opening his fist.

"They're magic," I said, spreading my palm next to Willie's.

"Mexican jumping beans," Doris Ann said, extending her hand.

"They're magic," I repeated.

Stewart dropped his canvas bag onto the sidewalk. "Those are Mexican jumping beans," he said matter-of-factly.

"Yeah," I said, catching my breath. "Watch 'em jump. You can
make a wish and get anything you want."

Stewart shoved his hands into his pockets. "Who told you that?"

"Sylvester," I answered.

Stewart rolled his eyes. "Those aren't magic beans."

"They're Mexican jumping beans!" I shouted.

"Yeah," Stewart said, "but they're *not* magic."

Our faces fell, and we backed away from Stewart.

"They're *not* magic," he said again.

I walked up to him and held out the beans. "Watch 'em jump," I
said.

"There's a worm in there," Stewart said. "That's what makes 'em
jump."

"Huh!" Willie shouted.

"Go ask Mom," Stewart said.

Doris Ann ran inside and came right back nodding her head.
"She says it's a worm."

"Darn," Willie whispered. Our hearts fell, and our shoulders sagged. The three of us sat on the front porch steps and rolled the beans onto the sidewalk at our feet. They jumped and wiggled.

"That *Sylvester*," I fumed.

Doris Ann slipped the wrappers from her jawbreakers and popped both of them into her mouth.

Realizing he had crushed our dreams, Stewart picked up a bean and rolled it around in his palm. "The worm eats the bean from the inside out," he said.

I didn't want Stewart to feel bad, so I picked up a bean and pretended to be more interested than I really was. I turned the bean over and over. There were no holes or cracks in the shell. "How does it get in there?" I asked.

"I don't know," Stewart said, holding one up to the light and squinting as if to see through it.

Doris Ann made a loud sucking noise, and I glanced up. She looked like a chipmunk. I thought of trading her all five of my jumping beans for one of her wet jawbreakers, but I knew she'd never go for it.

Stewart sat down beside me. Trying to cheer us up, he said, "You know, these beans do have magic. If you watch them long enough, the worm eats the bean and it turns into a butterfly. That's magic, don't you think?"

Willie groaned. "We've got thirteen worthless beans and no candy."

"And pretty soon," I added, "we won't have the beans."

Doris Ann sucked noisily on her jawbreakers.

Stewart scooped up a handful of jumping beans. "They are swell, though, don't you think?"

I put one in my palm and watched it wiggle. "Yeah," I said.

The screen door slammed behind us, and our brother John, who was just five, came out and sat down beside Stewart.

"Whatcha got?" he asked.

"Mexican jumping beans," Stewart said, dropping one onto John's palm.

It wiggled. "Wow," he shouted, lifting his hand for a closer inspection. The bean wiggled again. "Wow," he said, and without taking his eyes off the bean, marched inside to show it to Mother.

Stewart dropped his head, nodding, letting us know that John had understood the magic of a Mexican jumping bean without any hope for granted wishes. He studied the beans for a minute, then bumped my shoulder with his and smiled broadly. "So, what were you going to wish for?" he asked.

PART 1

1973– '83

dreaming through the twilight

"You ought to join the military, Southpaw," my dad said. I smiled at his term of endearment, *Southpaw*. When I was a little girl, he'd tried to force me to be right-handed by tying my left hand behind my back when I wrote. At some point, sensing futility, he'd given it up and now seemed to enjoy my left-handedness. We were sitting on the back steps. He smoked while I sketched the pine trees behind our house, drawing with an ink pen in a spiral notebook that was supposed to be filled with notes for my upcoming American history final.

"We're pulling out of Vietnam," he said. "You wouldn't have to worry about going to war." He sighed. "Anyway, it'd get you out of this godforsaken place." He dropped his cigarette, snuffed it out with the toe of his shoe, and sauntered down the steps—heading to the bar.

I watched him throw a hand briefly into the air and climb into his car. I waved back, knowing he'd come home drunk and ready for a fight. I worried that his mild suggestion to join the military might turn into a demand come midnight. I cringed at the thought of how my present situation—graduating without any prospects—might turn into a salient point once he'd had a few drinks. The previous Friday night, he'd come home from the bar, and before Mother had time to turn on the lights, he started shouting, *Barbara, when are you going to get a job?!* The fact that I was still in high school, didn't own a car, and lived miles from the bus stop didn't seem to enter into the question.

I tossed my spiral notebook onto the porch and climbed onto the glider of my baby sister Janet's swing set. I threw my legs over the backseat, flipped upside down, and closed my eyes. My long hair swept the grass as I pumped the swing into motion. I let my mind wander. Within seconds my favorite daydream filtered in. *I'm at the opening of my first art show. Gorgeous paintings line the gallery walls: water lilies, several views of a haystack, bright sunflowers* (images mentally swiped from my mother's art books). *Suddenly a New York City gallery owner arrives. She's wearing a black dress with a bright red pillbox hat and matching lipstick. Thrilled with my artwork, she throws her arms around me. "You are brilliant," she declares. "I'm taking you straight to the Big Apple."*

Just then someone climbed onto the other seat of the glider. "What are you smiling about?" Doris Ann asked.

"I'm not smiling," I said, opening my eyes and glaring at my younger sister. She flipped upside down and put her head next to mine. "You wanna walk down to Junior's house?" she asked.

Junior, our closest neighbor, lived a mile away. "It's too hot," I said, shrugging my shoulders, irritated. "And I'm trying to *think*."

"Think about what?"

"About joining the military," I lied, closing my eyes again. My daydream instantly changed to olive drab. *I snatch up a rolling grenade, toss it away, and fire off a round, saving my platoon. For my heroism, I'm stationed back in the States and given a job creating a new, sharper design for the military camouflage uniforms. The pattern I create is used universally for uniforms, helicopters, and vehicles.*

Doris Ann threw her hands behind her head. "When you join the military, I'll have a bedroom all to myself."

Just then Willie chased John around the side of the house with a water balloon. John, screaming his head off, climbed over Doris Ann and me and kept running. Willie did the same.

"Get out of here!" I shouted, slapping at them as they dashed away. I squeezed my eyes shut. *Suddenly a New York gallery owner arrives. She's wearing a black leather pantsuit and love beads with a big peace sign.* Happy with this daydream, I smiled to myself.

I heard the screen door slam and opened one eye. Mother stood on the porch. As the glider swept back and forth, I could see half of her, then all of her, then half again. My baby sister Janet, who was four, came out and caught hold of Mother's skirt at the curve of her hip. Like a snapping turtle, she'd hold that fabric in her fist until it thundered. But from the stormy expression on Mother's face, thunder was on the way. I waited for her to say my name before opening my other eye.

"Barbara," she called, "do you want to wash the supper dishes or play with Janet?"

I opened my eyes and winked at Janet. She laughed, knowing the answer, and bounded down the stairs and jumped into my arms.

"What were you smiling about?" she asked.

Doris Ann scooted over and I pulled Janet onto the glider. "I'm smiling at you," I said.

I joined the Navy—because the uniforms were bell-bottoms. But when I went for my physical, the first thing the doctor checked was my heartbeat. He put the stethoscope on my chest and moved it around. "Have you had rheumatic fever?" he asked.

"When I was thirteen," I answered.

He shook his head. "She's out," he shouted. A nurse came to escort me out of the examining room.

"Wait," I cried. "I've got to get in." But the doctor waved me away.

Months went by. I helped Mother look after Janet, helped her wash clothes in the wringer washer, weeded the garden, played horseshoes with Willie and Doris Ann, taught my youngest brother, John, to walk all the way around the house on an empty fifty-five-gallon drum, sketched the pine trees. I spent more time than ever daydreaming, but when I opened my eyes and left the dream behind, I couldn't see a future at all. My life had come to a standstill.

My neighbor introduced me to Rudy. He was in the Army, stationed at Fort McClellan, a military installation on the outskirts of Anniston. "You're tall," he said, eyeing me from head to toe.

"Yeah," I said, embarrassed.

"My ex-wife was short," Rudy said. Then he asked me if I'd ever been with a man. "I'm looking for a *pure* woman this time."

We got married at the chapel out at Fort McClellan. Dad was supposed to give the bride away, but the military police at the front gate arrested him for public intoxication. My older brother David had to stand in for him. (My oldest brother, Stewart, who would have been next in line for the honor, had joined the Marines.) After the wedding ceremony, the guards called the chapel. As a wedding gift, they were releasing Dad without a fine. We could pick him up on the way out if someone sober was available to drive his car home.

"I could hardly be called drunk," Dad said as the guards helped him into the backseat of our car. Mother turned away and wouldn't speak.

I was glad to see him, glad he wasn't in jail. "Dad, you missed the wedding," I said, flashing my ring in his face.

Dad nudged Mother. "If I'd known they considered a few beers to be intoxicated, I wouldn't have wasted twenty bucks on this monkey suit."

awakening

Rudy took my arm and guided me through the hospital corridor at the Fort McClellan military base, avoiding contact with other military personnel as if we were dodging bullets. He and I had been sitting in the car until a room was available so that I wouldn't be "gawked at" by the GIs in the hospital waiting room. I tried not to look at them, young men and women dressed in crisp uniforms the color of ripe green olives, but the uniforms tugged at my heartstrings. Six months earlier, I had hoped to be wearing one rather than ironing someone else's.

Rudy guided me into the examining room and the nurse sent him away. He left reluctantly, as if I'd somehow created a conspiracy to be alone with another man.

I put on a faded cotton gown, sat on the cold examining table and flipped the thin sheet over my legs, cringing at the thought of a pelvic examination. I lifted my feet into the air and pulled the sheet up so I could admire my red-painted toenails. I'd painted them the night before the appointment, hoping they'd distract the doctor from my private parts.

The doctor came into the exam room, reading my chart. Without looking up, he asked, "What seems to be the problem?"

"I can't get rid of the stomach flu," I said.

"You're probably pregnant," he said.

"No, I can't be," I said. "My husband is sterile."

The doctor lowered the clipboard and looked at me. "Did he tell you that?"

I nodded, then blushed at the incredulous look on his face. He laughed out loud and left the exam room sniggering and shaking his head. As soon as the door closed, I pulled the thin sheet over my head. Half an hour later he came back with the test results. "It's positive," he said. I waited for him to say something more—or laugh again. But he simply cocked his head in my direction, and said, "You can get dressed," and left.

I pulled on my blue jeans, fuming that Mother hadn't told me more about the birds and the bees. She must have thought my older sister, Alice, would tell me, or maybe one of my older brothers. And they had filled me in on the gist of it, but mostly through dirty jokes and pictures David had torn from his friends' girlie magazines. I had no idea what *positive* meant. I got dressed and went out to the waiting room. Rudy shot me a questioning look.

I shrugged. "He says it's *positive.*"

Rudy jumped from his chair. "It's positive! It's positive!" he shouted, dancing around the room. "I'm gonna have a baby boy! A baby boy!" He twirled me around. I laughed, relieved to know what *positive* meant and relieved at Rudy's response. He twirled me until he noticed the young men sitting around the room were also enjoying the moment. Rudy didn't believe that *any* man could be trusted around *any* woman, and vice versa. It was as simple as that. He pulled me toward the exit, but he was still smiling.

Rudy loaded his fishing tackle into the trunk of his car. "You're gonna be a mother," he said. "You'd better get used to staying at home."

I crossed my arms. "When will you be back?" I asked, hoping he wasn't leaving for the entire weekend.

"I'll be back when I get back," he said, slamming the trunk. He escorted me up the stairs to our second-floor apartment, unlocked the dead bolt on the door, let me in, and locked it again. Through the door, he said, "I'll be back tonight. Late. Don't wait up."

I leaned against the door. "Okay. I love you."

"Me too," Rudy said. But I could tell by the echo that he was already heading down the stairs.

I didn't have a telephone, the apartment had been cleaned, and Rudy's military uniforms had been ironed. I'd already drawn pictures on my entire supply of notebook paper and had even sketched the scene from the kitchen window on the brown paper bags from the grocery store. I flopped into the rocking chair and started to cry, burying my face in a pillow, thinking, *This is worse than living with Dad.*

I fell asleep, and startled when someone knocked on the door.

"It's me, Alice," my older sister said.

I ran to the door, delighted. "Hey!"

"Is Rudy home?"

"No."

"Well, let me in."

"I can't. I don't have the key."

"Oh, for Christ's sake," Alice said. "All right. I'll go around back."

A few minutes later she pulled her beat-up Chevy Impala under the bedroom window, flattening the holly bushes that ran along the back of the building, and honked the horn three times. I opened the window and waved. The first floor of our apartment house was partially belowground, so our apartment window wasn't that high up.

Alice got out of her car and looked up at me. "I'm going to the Laundromat. You want to go?"

I shoved the window all the way open, sat on the sill, and threw my legs out. Alice climbed onto the hood, then onto the roof of her car. She jumped up and down to make sure it wouldn't cave in, but she weighed so little the car barely moved. "Okay, Lil' Sister," she threw out her arms, "jump."

I leapt into the air and landed with a thud right in the middle of the roof. Alice threw her arms around me to keep me from falling.

"I've got three loads," she said as we slid onto the hood and jumped to the ground. "Probably take a couple hours. You sure he won't come home while we're gone?"

"Yeah," I said. "Pretty sure."

She shook her head in disgust as we climbed into the car.

As the clothes churned in the heavy washers, Alice smoked cigarettes and filled me in on my brothers and sisters, skipping herself but otherwise going down the line in birth order: "Stewart comes home from Okinawa in three months. David's out of boot camp in one. Willie's still running that Trans Am up and down the road like a bat outta hell. Doris Ann's got a date Friday night with some new guy. John's driving Mother crazy ripping up the driveway on David's motorcycle, and here's a couple of drawings from Janet." Alice reached into her purse and pulled out two sheets of folded notebook paper. "They're portraits of you. Pregnant." Alice laughed and flicked ashes into the air.

Janet had been born when I was twelve years old. It was like getting a real live baby doll for Christmas. Since I'd gotten married and moved out, she'd been sending me pictures, most of them drawn with crayons. I unfolded the notebook paper and smiled. There I was—tall and skinny, with a bubble on my tummy.

Alice leaned over to take a look. "You look like a broom straw that swallowed a BB."

I chuckled, folded the drawings, and handed them back to Alice. "Will you hold on to them? Until the next time I see you and Rudy is with me?"

Alice took the drawings, shoved them back into her purse, and took a long pull from her cigarette. She blew the smoke into the air slowly, lost in her thoughts. When she finally spoke, I didn't know whether she was talking about my husband or hers. "He's worse than Dad," she said.

After we finished washing clothes, Alice drove back under the bedroom window, and we climbed back on top of the car. She cupped her hands together and I slipped my foot into her palms.

"You ready?" she said.

I nodded.

"One, two, three." And she hoisted me up. I snatched the windowsill and flexed my toes so that my tennis shoes hit the rough bricks, protecting my knees. I made a mental note not to wear shorts the next time. I lifted my foot and felt around until I found a row of protruding bricks, slipped my toes onto them, and eased up until my butt stuck in the air and I fell through the open window onto the floor. I jumped up and waved at Alice down below. She waved back and hopped off the car.

"I'll see you in a few days," she shouted.

One day Rudy's military friend Bob stopped by our apartment—and he brought his pregnant wife, Diane. Diane was free to explore Fort McClellan in search of entertainment. Before she got pregnant, she had joined a bowling team and taken archery. In the few times we had seen them, Diane had told me all about her adventures. In return, I showed her my drawings and told her my dream of becoming an artist.

Diane dragged me into the kitchen. "Get the guys a beer so we can talk," she said.

I took two beers into the living room and came back into the kitchen.

Diane pulled two glasses from the cabinet and turned on the water in the kitchen sink. "There's an art shop," she whispered.

I glanced at Rudy, then back at Diane. "Where?"

"Out at the Fort. I'll come get you tomorrow."

"I can't go," I whispered.

"Yes, you can," she said, pinching me on the arm.

Fort McClellan was absolutely forbidden. Rudy had told me over and over, *Never go out there. Soldiers will sleep with anyone!* And since he was one, he knew. I wasn't the least bit interested in the men. I wanted to make art. Any kind of art. And classes and supplies at the art shop were free to soldiers' wives. All you needed was a military ID card.

Diane drove a new black pickup truck. The roof of the cab was considerably higher than the roof of Alice's old Chevy, making the jump from our bedroom window much easier.

At the art shop, Diane pulled me along by the sleeve, stopping at the class schedule hanging on the bulletin board. "Ceramics," she said. "That's what we're going to take first. I love clay."

I didn't argue. I felt pretty much like clay myself, unshaped. I had been telling everyone all my life that I was going to be an artist, but other than the drawing lessons my own mother had given me, I hadn't really been exposed to art making. I looked around the military art shop and my hands tingled. The room was filled with art supplies: two kilns, and a huge stack of plaster slip molds for making dishes and whatnots, little jars of glazes, pencils, paper, paints, brushes. One side of the room was set up with a dozen easels. Several Army wives listened as an instructor explained how to paint a rainy, watercolor sky. I leaned against the wall and put my hands on my cheeks; heat radiated from my palms.

In a few short months, I had made a bowl, salt and pepper shakers, two happy gnomes with long beards, and a Christmas tree with a tiny light on the tip of each branch. I couldn't take my treasures home, so I stored them in a locker at the art shop. For weeks I had been waiting my turn to use the slip mold to make an elaborate chess set. The king stood four inches tall. He wore a crown and a long brocade cloak. His queen wore a matching crown and a formfitting gown. The knights rode horses, and each pawn held a saber and shield. It was the most difficult mold in the shop, and I couldn't wait to try my hand at it. I had decided to paint each piece realistically, faces and all, rather than simply painting one set white and the other black.

Diane stood on the roof of her pickup truck, cupping her hands around her mouth. "Barbara!" she shouted. "Your chess set came out of the kiln today."

I opened the window and leaned out. "None of the pieces broke?"

"Not a one!" Diane shouted. "They're gorgeous!" She waved her hands. "Come on. Come on. You gotta see."

I climbed through the window and jumped onto the roof of the truck. Diane grabbed me when I landed. "Your husband's an idiot," she said. "You've got no business jumping out of a window when you're six months pregnant. You know it won't be long before we won't be able to do this."

A shiver ran down my spine. Lately, my blue jeans wouldn't zip anymore. To keep them up, I tied a ribbon through the belt loops and covered my exposed belly with a big shirt. I felt invincible and hadn't considered the impact the short jump might have on the baby.

When we arrived at the art shop, a crowd had gathered around my chess set. The instructor had emptied the kiln and set the chess pieces on the matching ceramic board. He smiled at me. "I've already had an offer for three hundred dollars, Barbara. Do you want to sell it?"

I blushed.

"You can always make another," he said.

A vision of selling one-of-a-kind chess sets entered my mind, but immediately faded. I knew I wouldn't be able to make even one more set. Diane was right, I shouldn't be jumping out the window while pregnant. I shouldn't be jumping out the window at all. I wrapped the chess set in newspaper and packed it in a box with the rest of my treasures. Diane refused to help me, believing that if she pouted, I'd reconsider and jump out of the window for at least another week or two.

"Can you run me over to my mom's house?" I asked.

"Sure," she said, flipping her dark hair behind her ears. "Are you going to give all this stuff to your mom?"

"No, Rudy would see it, and he'd know where it came from. I'm going to hide it there, and eventually I'll give it all to the baby."

Two months later, Rudy and I moved into a little house on Coldwater Pump Road—just a quarter of a mile from Bob and Diane. Rudy had his brother help move the big pieces of furniture into the house, then they stacked the boxes in the living room and left. And this time, he didn't lock me in. He must have felt that no man would be interested in a woman who was eight months pregnant.

A few minutes later Diane knocked on my door. When I threw open the door, she said, "I saw Rudy's car go by." I stood in the doorway transfixed, unsure of what to do next. I was really glad to see my friend. I had been terribly lonely. Since I'd quit jumping out the window, my days were filled with ironing Rudy's military uniforms, spit-shining his jump boots, cleaning house, and cooking. I was bored out of my mind.

"Well," she said, "are you going to invite me in?"

I stepped back and waved her inside. "Of course," I said, glancing down the road to make sure Rudy hadn't turned around. Diane knew that I had been forbidden to go to Fort McClellan, but she didn't know that I wasn't allowed visitors. "Would you like some tea?" I asked.

We sipped tea and traded pregnancy stories, but my ears stayed alert to the sound of Rudy's car coming down the road. Diane was completely oblivious.

"I've got the cutest crib," she said. "It's white with blue moons painted on it. You gotta come see it." She stood up and pulled on my arm. "Come on. Let's go take a look."

I didn't know where Rudy had gone or when he'd be back. Leaving was risky. "What if Rudy comes home while I'm gone?" I asked.

"My house is just down the street. You'll be back in a flash."

My face must have shown my concern.

"It'll be fine!" she assured me. "You're just going to look at a crib."

I left a note explaining where I had gone and left the front door unlocked so I could get back in.

Diane had a complete nursery set up for her baby: crib, dresser, changing station, rocking chair. On the dresser and in the crib were stuffed toys and rattles. I picked up a rattle with a football-shaped orb. Diane rolled her eyes. "Bob keeps buying this stuff. He's hoping for a boy."

I felt a twinge of jealousy. Rudy hadn't bought anything for our baby. Diane read my mind. "Here," she said, picking out a red lollipop rattle. "You take this one with you. I've got too many already."

I shook the rattle and listened to the faint musical chime.

"Oh," she said, waddling into the other room, "I've got something else for you." She came back with a faded blue maternity blouse and matching pants. "I noticed you needed these," she said, tugging on the ribbon tied around my waist. I hugged the outfit and pressed my face into the soft fabric.

Twenty minutes later, Diane took me home. As we drove up, Rudy tossed an armload of my clothes out the front door. My jewelry box lay broken on the steps, and art books were scattered on the yard. I picked up my favorite shirt and laid it across my arm with the maternity outfit and tried the door. It was locked. "Rudy?" I cried, turning the doorknob back and forth.

The door jerked open and caught on the safety chain. Rudy peeked through the space. "Get your clothes and get the hell out of my yard!" he shouted.

"Rudy, we went to look at Diane's new crib."

"I don't give a damn where you were, you whore. Get out of my yard." He slammed the door and flipped the lock.

"This is ridiculous," Diane said.

I banged on the door and waited. A moment later, we could hear Rudy loading his shotgun.

"Let's get out of here," Diane said. She pulled me to the car, shoved me into the passenger seat, and drove back to her house.

Diane's husband listened as she told him what had happened. He looked at me with a dismal expression on his face, then tugged on Diane's sleeve. "Could I speak with you privately?" he asked. They went into the kitchen.

"We can't just keep her," he said. "It's not like she's a puppy that followed you home. She's a grown woman. A *pregnant* grown woman. She's gotta go back to her husband."

I sat in the living room and stared out the window, miserably listening to their conversation, and trying to think of where I could go. Diane reluctantly made her way back into the living room, but before she could tell me I had to leave, I saw Rudy's car turn into the driveway. I wiped the tears from my face and smiled.

"He's here," I said, flooded with relief. I gathered my clothes, hugged Diane, and dashed out of the door, delighted that he had come for me. Rudy climbed from the car, and I smiled, hoping he would smile back. Instead he snatched the clothes out of my hand and tossed them to the ground, then grabbed my upper arms and shook me as hard as he could, snapping my head back and forth. "What did you think you were doing?" he shouted. "I've told you a thousand times! *Never* leave without permission, and nobody comes in the house when I'm not home! Who else has been there?"

"Nobody," I cried.

"There's no telling what you've been up to! Even *pregnant*, I can't leave you alone for a minute! Where else have you been?" He let go of my arms and slapped me, and I fell against the car.

Rudy grabbed my hair and shouted in my face, "Who else have you let in the house?!"

"Nobody," I cried.

He let go of my hair. "Nobody?" he shouted. "How do I know this baby is even mine?"

I curled over the hood of the car as a sharp pain ran down my back. Rudy grabbed my arm and tried to make me stand up, but I sank to the ground as another pain shot through me.

Diane's husband came out and stood on his front steps. He was a small man. Rudy was twice his size, and twice as mean. He put his hands in his pockets and looked embarrassed. "Is she all right?" he asked.

Rudy turned and pointed at him. "This is none of your damn business." He grabbed my arm again, and I hunkered down.

"This baby's moving," I said.

Rudy stood over me.

"Really," I said, pushing against my round belly, "this baby's moving."

Suddenly Rudy was picking me up and carefully putting me in the car. I curled into a ball as he climbed into the driver's seat and sped the car toward town. He brushed my curly hair away from my face, and I looked up at him. He smiled as if nothing at all had happened and stepped on the gas pedal.

"Are we having a baby?" he asked.

"I don't know. It hurts. It hurts real bad."

"Hot damn, we're having a baby!" Rudy shouted. "My own baby boy!"

I curled up and pushed my back against the car seat, hoping it would ease the pain. It felt like someone was stabbing me in the lower back with a knife. Still, I didn't believe I was in labor.

🦎

The emergency room nurse took my vital signs and pointed out the bruises on my arms to the doctor. He admitted me without saying a word. As soon as I was in my room, Rudy ran down to the flower shop and brought back a bright pink rose in a thin vase. He kissed me on the cheek and put it on the nightstand.

Gleefully, he said, "I'm gonna go get my brother. I'll be right back." And out the door he went, almost knocking over the nurse as she came in. She watched him trot down the hall to the elevator, then looked at me. "This baby's not coming today," she said. "But we figured you could use a rest."

"Thanks," I said.

"And I'm sending someone up to see you."

A few minutes later, a black woman the size of a mountain came in and stood over me, musing. Finally she said, "I'm from Social Services." Without further introduction, she said, "You got a mama?"

"Yes, ma'am," I answered.

"She a good woman?"

"Yes, ma'am."

She nodded. Her eyes drifted to my swollen belly, to the bruises on my arms, and then back to my red-streaked face. "Why don't you go home to your mama?"

I looked at my folded hands, opened them as if to set some small thing free, then clasped them together again. All the women I knew were ruled, and often abused, by their husbands. I thought that was marriage. Yet I ached with a desperate feeling that wouldn't go away. I wanted to do something with my life. And I knew it would never happen as long as I was married to this man. I had already tried to go back home, months earlier, when the sorrow of giving up the art shop had overwhelmed me with tears, but Dad had pitched a fit and sent me back to my husband.

"I can't," I said. "My dad's embarrassed because I'm pregnant." Having said it out loud, I blushed.

"Uh-huh," the woman said. "He like babies okay?"

I nodded.

"He just don't like the idea of how they get here, huh?" The woman put her huge hands on her hips. "Listen, I'm not telling you what to do. I'm only saying what *I'd* do, if I was you." She nodded toward the rose. "I'd go back to that *so-called husband,* and I'd do everything I had to do not to make him mad for a few weeks until my baby got born. And as soon as I was strong enough, I'd take my new baby and I'd go home to my mama. That's what I'd do."

The fact that I wouldn't be pregnant forever hadn't entered my mind. I counted in my head—five or six weeks before I could escape. I looked up and caught a faint smile on the woman's face. I returned it and said, "Yes, ma'am."

escaping

Mother brought in a box of my things and stood in the middle of the room I'd be sharing with my youngest sister, Janet. "Where do you want this?" she asked.

The side of the box read *Art Supplies*. It didn't contain much because Rudy had destroyed almost everything I'd held dear. He'd ripped up my clothes, torn drawings, snapped brushes, and smashed the two life-size clay cats I'd just brought home from the art shop.

The cats had been my way of giving our relationship one more chance. I brought them home, still warm from the kiln, bisque-fired but not yet glazed. One was curled into a ball, sleeping; the other sat up, wide-eyed, with his tail wrapped around his body, the tip resting on his front paws. I put them on the coffee table.

When Rudy drove up, I met him at the door. I held our newborn son, Jason, in one arm and threw the other toward the clay cats as if to say *ta-da*.

"See what I can do, Rudy," I said, feigning glee. Rudy's mouth fell open and his car keys dropped to the floor.

"I don't hunt for guys when I go out to the art shop, Rudy. It's just Army wives. You can come see for yourself."

That was as far as I got. Rudy picked up the lamp and, in one movement, jerked the plug out of the wall and snatched off the shade; using the lamp base like a baseball bat, he smashed the clay cats to dust. If I hadn't been holding baby Jason, he might have turned the lamp on me. Instead, he started smashing everything in sight. As he

stormed through the house, I ran next door and convinced our neighbor to drive Jason and me to my parents' house.

Mother gently rattled the box. "Barbara?"

I looked around the crowded room. We had already pushed Jason's
crib into the corner and shoved boxes underneath it. Janet's clothes
and stuffed toys had been tossed inside it. What was left of my
clothes had been thrown over the piled-high chair.

I sat down on the bed and eased Jason into the middle. "Just put it
on the back porch, Mom," I said. "There's not any room left in here."

Mother sat the box right in the narrow path that led to the door.
"Your sketchbooks are in here," she said, opening the flaps. "And art
pencils. You don't want these things to get ruined if it rains."

She reached into the box and picked up the Polaroid camera Rudy
had given me for Christmas. Somehow it had survived his wrath.

"Come on," she said. "Let's take some pictures of my new grandbaby."

She took several shots. We tacked them on the bedroom wall and
stared at them as they developed.

Mother smiled and pointed out the red cherub lips forming before
our eyes. "He's a doll," Mother said. She put the camera back in the
box and left me alone to study the developing photographs. I liked
them, but Jason seemed far more beautiful than the flat, pink shape
that crowded those small squares. I climbed onto the bed and studied
his sleeping face. The camera hadn't captured the beauty of his eyes, or
the mystery in the shape of his brow. I reached into the box of art supplies and found a pencil. On an old envelope, I drew his head. Scribbled in the eyes, nose, and mouth. Drawing let my mind slip sideways,
and I wondered if my mother had ever looked so closely at me. After
all, when I was born, she already had three children. Did she watch
me breathe as I slept? Wait for that moment when my eyes would
bounce open, only to fall closed again like a drifting summer leaf?

I looked up to see if I'd gotten his likeness, and now he stared back
at me. I gasped. This tiny baby looked at me as if he knew all my
secrets. I put the pencil down, picked him up, and buried my face in

his tender neck and baby smell. I couldn't believe my luck. He wanted me and only me to hold him, sing to him, rock him to sleep. Nobody else had ever chosen me above all others. I held him up and gazed into his deep, round eyes and wondered what else he knew—and whether he would teach it to me.

All the love-starved people living in that sad old house melted under Jason's spell, but it was still my responsibility to raise him, and I had no idea how I was going to do that on my own. When he was five weeks old, I bought an old junk car and took a job as a dental assistant, but I worried about leaving him. I trusted my mother to take care of him, but Rudy had threatened to steal him away, and I was terrified that he'd succeed.

One morning Dad woke me up at the crack of dawn. "Your car's gone," he said.

I jumped out of bed and ran out the front door. "Rudy stole my car!" I cried. Then fear shot through me. I ran back inside to make sure Jason was still in his crib. My dad was a step ahead of me and held my sleeping baby out to me when I ran into the room. I eased him onto my shoulder and he started to whimper. I bounced and patted his back.

"What am I going to do, Dad?" I cried.

"Don't worry about it. You'll get another car."

Tears welled in my eyes. "What if he steals Jason?" I whispered.

Just then Mother spoke up. She was standing in the doorway holding a cast-iron skillet, about to start breakfast. "He is *not* going to steal Jason," she said. "Your father is here, and I'm here. And besides, what would he do with a baby? He took the car because he knew the police wouldn't do anything about it. But he'd go to jail for kidnapping." She held the skillet out as if considering the weight of it. "If he lived to go to jail."

Months went by and I didn't hear from Rudy. Then one day I ran into him at the grocery store. When I saw him, I covered Jason's head with his blanket and headed for the exit, hoping to escape. I made it out the door before Rudy caught up with me and grabbed my arm. He reached as if to take Jason from me and I started to scream. Jason screamed too. Dad had been waiting for me in the car, and suddenly he was there.

"You don't want to do that," Dad said.

Rudy let go of me and took a step back. "I just want to hold my son," he said.

Dad's eyes narrowed. "Start paying your child support and you can hold him whenever you want." He indicated for me to leave, and I ran across the parking lot and locked myself in his car. Dad said something else to Rudy but I couldn't hear it. When he climbed into the car a few minutes later, he said, "You won't have to worry about him anymore."

Still, I felt the threat like a boogeyman, something bad that lurked out there in the dark.

Since I didn't own a car anymore, Dad had to drop me at my job on his way to work every day. Saving enough money for another car was much harder than I had imagined. Even though I lived with my parents, I hardly made enough to get me through each week.

Yet, I was happier and more hopeful than I had ever been. With Jason in my arms, I felt an unparalleled awakening. I prized the evenings when, aching with exhaustion, I would collapse into the rocker with my baby. And as he played with my ears, his eyelids dropping into slumber, I'd close my eyes too and, fortified with baby love, slip once again into the daydreams his father had put on hold.

I dreamed of the female artists Frida Kahlo and Georgia O'Keeffe. I imagined the long and arduous but magical path that would eventually lead me to such artistic greatness. I envisioned myself in art school, a loaded paintbrush behind each ear, intent on my work. Behind my closed lids, O'Keeffe's dramatic flower and cow-skull paintings became mine, luring entranced crowds unable to turn themselves away from my vibrant colors and ingenious compositions.

maverick

When Jason was eight months old, I bought another car. A 1968 candy-apple-red Maverick. Dad helped me choose it from the used-car lot. Somehow, that bit of assistance gave him squatter's rights, and he began taking my Maverick to his favorite drinking spot so the police wouldn't recognize him by the car he was driving. The local police knew my dad well, Stewart Karl Moss, S.K. for short; they played cat and mouse regularly.

One Friday night Dad didn't come home. The next morning Mother, Alice, and I sat on the front porch swing in our nightgowns, worrying.

Jason rested contentedly on Mother's lap, and baby sister, Janet, sprawled on the porch with Alice's little boys, Darrell and Chris, piecing together a jigsaw puzzle.

"I'm glad he doesn't have my car this time," Alice said, pushing the swing with her toes. "I can't afford another ninety-dollar fine."

"Somebody would've called by this time if he'd had a wreck, wouldn't they?" I asked.

Mother stood Jason on her lap and jiggled him to make him laugh, but then she looked away. Her brow furrowed and she said, "He could be in trouble. We better go look for him."

"Maybe he's passed out down at Stewart's house," Alice said.

"Maybe he's in jail," I said.

Mother's face clouded. "We better go look for him," she said again, only this time she was interrupted by the wail of approaching sirens. Alice stopped the swing. We all sat up straighter. Jason cocked his head, and the other kids dropped their puzzle pieces. Mother climbed out of the swing, everybody jumped to their feet, and we edged to the end of the porch. As the sirens got closer, Janet, Darrell, and Chris clapped their hands over their ears. Suddenly my car, going ninety to nothing, skidded onto our dirt road, rousing an impressive cloud of red dust that followed it all the way up the driveway.

Janet pointed. "There's Dad!"

Alice and I snatched the kids out of the way just as Dad swung the Maverick into the yard and slid to a stop inches from the porch where we were standing. Two police cars skidded in right behind him, sirens screaming, gravel and red dirt flying.

Dad threw his arm out the open window and banged on the car door. "I beat you, by God!" he shouted. "I beat both of you! You're no match for me!"

The sirens screeched and then died. The bubble lights on top of the patrol cars flashed blinding blue and red. The officer in the first car leaned out his open window and shouted, "All right, S.K., we've got you."

"Like hell!" Dad shouted. "I'm in my own goddamn yard." He laughed and waved at us. Marveling, we waved back.

The officer in charge climbed out of his patrol car. His partner eased out of the other door, pulled a pair of handcuffs from his belt, and leaned against the hood of the patrol car, waiting. The officer driving the second patrol car rolled down the window and stuck out his head.

"You need more backup?" he shouted.

The officer in charge waved him away. "Nope. This'll just take a minute." He walked to the Maverick, and Dad hooted. "You boys need to take some driving lessons. Can't beat an old coot like me!" He doubled over with laughter.

"Get out of the car, S.K."

"No, sir. I beat you. I'm sitting on home ground. There ain't nothing you can do."

I looked at Mother. "Is that true?"

Mother nodded, a bemused grin on her face. Alice looked at me, and we smiled. A chance to be on the winning side made us giddy. Dad was always getting in trouble with the police, and we knew them to be downright nasty most of the time. This time, it seemed, Dad had gotten over on them.

"You mean he can stay in that car until he sobers up?" Alice asked.

Jason pointed gleefully at the flashing red and blue lights as Mother bounced him. "They can't arrest him unless he puts his foot on the ground," she said.

"Don't get out of the car, Dad!" Alice shouted.

"Don't get out of the car, Dad!" I shouted.

Still laughing, Dad hung out the window and pointed at Janet. "There's my baby girl! The last of the Mohicans." He waved both hands in the air. Janet blushed and waved back.

"Hi, Daddy," she said, smiling broadly. "I can see you."

"I see you too, honey." Dad waved at Darrell and Chris. "Hi, boys. When you grow up, I'll teach you to drive!" And he burst out laughing again. "Southpaw," he said to me, "your car runs like a top!"

The officer frowned. "Get out of the car, S.K."

"Not on your life," Dad said, and drummed a little ditty on the steering wheel.

The officer pushed on the back of his hat until it fell forward and almost covered his eyes. He tilted his head back so he could see. "You know we got you, S.K." He started counting on his fingers. "Driving without a license. Driving while intoxicated. Speeding. Reckless driving. Failure to pull over." He paused, looked over at us, took off his hat, and addressed Mother. "Tell him, Dorris. Tell him to get out of the car and come along peacefully."

Mother looked at her bare feet, then back to the officer. "I can't tell him anything," she said almost cheerfully. "Never have been able to."

The officer shook his head and put his hat back on, adjusting it and readjusting it as if stalling for time. He took a deep breath and blew it out. "Make it easy on us all, S.K., and get out of the car."

"Don't do it, Dad!" the kids shouted.

"Not a chance," Dad said.

Alice and I laughed out loud. "Don't do it, Dad! Don't do it!"

Angry, the officer opened the car door. Dad threw his hands up. "You can't touch me and you know it," he said.

The officer slammed the door. He straightened, put his hands on his hips, and walked in a circle. "Fine," he said, and spit in the dirt. "Then we'll do it the hard way." He shouted to the policeman in the second patrol car, "Ron, call a wrecker. Call a wrecker, we're going to tow this car to the station with him in it!" He pointed to my candy-apple-red Maverick and said, "This car is now officially impounded!"

"Get out of the car, Dad!" I shouted. I stepped off the porch, put both hands on the hood, and bounced the car as if to shake him out. "Come on, Dad! Get out of the car!"

Everybody got quiet. Dad's face fell. He dropped his head, thinking it over, then glanced up at Mother.

From the porch, Mother said, "Come on, Stewart, get out of the car. She can't afford to get her car back. She's got to go to work on Monday."

Dad sat quietly for a few seconds, then opened the car door. As soon as his foot hit the dirt, the officer grabbed his arm. His partner walked over and snapped the handcuffs on his wrist.

"Daddy!" Janet cried.

"I'm all right, baby girl," Dad said, grinning.

Janet looked up, grabbed a fistful of Mother's nightgown, and tugged on it.

"It's all right, honey," Mother said. "We'll get dressed and go get him in a few minutes."

The officer in charge walked Dad toward the patrol car and pushed him into the backseat. Dad sniggered and called out to Mother, "I beat 'em, Dorris. Beat the pants off of 'em. Ten miles on a straight run. They didn't stand a chance." Mother bounced Jason. She still wore that bemused smile.

Before the officer shut the door, Dad yelled, "We did a beautiful job picking out that Maverick, Southpaw! That's one fine-running automobile."

sentinels

*D*ad worked hard all week and celebrated every Friday night at the American Legion. Weekends felt like war zones. Not long after I moved back home with my new baby, Alice moved in with her two sons. Mother usually made herself the object of Dad's drunken assaults, but with two grown daughters living under his roof, Dad had new targets for his anger.

"I want her out of here!" he yelled as he stumbled in the front door. It was the middle of the night, but everyone lay awake, waiting to find out who would be thrown out of the house this time. Alice was visiting her new boyfriend for the weekend, so I knew it would be me. Mother came into my bedroom and tapped me on the shoulder. "He wants to see you," she said. I nodded, climbed from bed, and pulled on a pair of blue jeans.

"Out!" he yelled as soon as I walked into the living room. "I raised you once. I'm not raising you again. Get out!"

"Where am I supposed to go?"

"I don't care where you go."

"What about Jason?"

"He's not going," Dad said matter-of-factly. "He's staying right here with his grandpa, where it's safe."

I threw my hands up and sighed. Happy and fearless, Jason had gone after my father's heart with reckless abandon. And won. Dad's booming voice had no effect on him whatsoever. Dad admired that and took the fledgling under his wing. They had their own secret language. Jason could stay; I had to go.

Dad waved his cigarette toward the couch, indicating that I should take a seat, so I flopped down. He sat in a chair and slid it closer to the couch, then leaned forward as he lit a cigarette. "Do you know what it costs to feed eleven people?" he asked.

It was pointless to answer. No matter what I said, Dad would throw me out eventually. And truthfully, I agreed with him on this particular issue. I *should* be living on my own.

"I don't make enough money, Dad," I explained. "By the time I pay my car payment and give Mom some money for babysitting, there's nothing left. I barely have enough left for baby food and gasoline for the week."

Dad blew smoke into the air and shouted, "So I've got to support my family and yours too?!"

I leaned forward, dropping my head into my hands, frustrated. Finally I looked at Dad. "My car will be paid for in eleven months. I'll start looking for an apartment the day I pay it off."

"Not next year! Now!" Dad shouted, indicating the door. "Out! Out! Out!"

I stood up and walked out onto the front porch. Dad locked the door behind me. I hopped off the porch into the yard and sifted the loose red dirt over my bare feet. It was still warm from the hot summer sun. Cicadas droned and fireflies beamed. The moon gleamed overhead, and in the woods, a pair of owls hooted back and forth. I walked across the dirt driveway and down a well-worn path to a grove of plum trees that were laden with fruit. Green with a hint of blush. I picked a handful and bit into one. The juice bit my tongue and I wished for some salt. I walked back to the house and sat in the porch swing, moving it back and forth with my toes. I ate the plums, one by one, alert for the sound of Jason crying. I didn't have anywhere to go, and even if I could collect Jason and think of somewhere, Dad had borrowed my car that night so my keys were in his pocket. And he knew that.

I rocked gently and thought about my situation. I liked living with my mother. She was kind and generous and knew babies like the back of her hand. Even Dad was familiar, tolerable most of the time. But recently Jason had started to walk. On his first birthday, I bought film for the Polaroid camera and took a few pictures around the house. In one photo, Jason is in his playpen on the porch, playing with a large kitchen spoon and one of Janet's broken dolls. Beside the playpen are a gas can with a rag stuffed in the spout, several greasy car parts, and a car battery. Several of the battery caps are scattered on the porch and the sun is glinting on the acid. In the background, my youngest brother, John, is standing on the seat of a motorcycle, arms stretched out like a balanced tightrope walker, riding down the driveway. As the Polaroids had developed before my eyes, the perils of this life also, suddenly, for the first time had come into focus. Mother had looked at the photos and seen it too. She said, "We must have angels watching over us."

I rocked the swing and bit into another plum. After that photo session, I'd taken the car battery to the dump. But as I looked around the porch now, even in the dark I spotted a number of hazardous objects that had taken its place: a rusty lawn-mower blade, porch paint, lug nuts, solvents. *Mother must be right,* I thought. *We have angels watching over us. Sentinels. And we keep them very busy.*

roses and Evening in Paris

When Jason was about two years old, I got a raise at work, and it was the break I needed. I didn't tell anyone and squirreled the money away. When I had saved enough for a deposit, I found an apartment that had been servants' quarters in an old house in Anniston. Two rooms, plus a closet that had been converted into a kitchen. I could stand by the stove and touch the walls on either side. The entire apartment was unbelievably small—and perfect. Hardwood floors, clean, close to work, and affordable.

I opened an account at the local furniture store, charged bunk beds, a rocking chair, and a love seat. I couldn't afford these things, but they were necessary. Jason and I both needed a place to sleep, and bunk beds conserved space—and time; when Jason cried during the night, I'd roll off the top bunk and slide onto the bottom one with him. The love seat was much less expensive than a sofa, and it fit the living room. And the rocking chair—well, I wasn't about to be anywhere without a rocker.

Our little apartment made a nice home. On my first weekend off, I painted a fake window on the kitchen wall above the sink so we'd have a view: green pastures with low mountains in the distance. And the view from our real windows was breathtaking, like a fairy tale— and fragrant. The woman who owned the house grew roses. The entire backyard was a labyrinth of bright reds, pinks, and yellows. Delighted, Jason learned the art of hide-and-seek in the crisscrossing rosebush passages.

It was a miracle that I'd found that apartment. But even as inexpensive as it was, I couldn't make ends meet. We were living on fried eggs for breakfast and macaroni and cheese for dinner. I'd already missed a payment at the furniture store when financial relief—of a sort—arrived. One of my girlfriends wanted to borrow my apartment to meet a married man.

"Please," she begged. "If we get caught, my husband will kill me. And his wife would probably kill me too."

I was speechless. I had never known a woman who cheated.

"Just this once," my friend said. "I love him. I'd get a divorce—but—you know, the kids."

I gave her my key. "Don't tell me who it is," I said. "And don't mess up my sheets."

"I won't," she said. "I promise, you'll never know we were there."

When I came home that evening, the house was just as I'd left it, except it smelled of the cologne Evening in Paris, and a twenty-dollar bill had been slipped under the sugar bowl.

Just this once turned into once a week—and $80 a month for me. Sometimes I felt guilty about it. Sometimes I felt like *I* was the one cheating. But the extra money made my furniture payment and bought biscuits, bacon, tea, chicken wings, dishwashing liquid, and shampoo. And the arrangement had some other odd perks. Occasionally I got flowers. They had obviously been given to my friend, and since she couldn't take them home, she left them with me. One day I found a pair of gold hoop earrings on the floor by the bed. Another day, a small, pearl-handled pocketknife. A white shirt button. Blue guitar pick. A Mercury-head dime.

I learned to like the smell of roses mixed with the lingering fragrance of Evening in Paris. I tried not to think about what would happen to me if they broke off their affair. I tried not to think about the fact that one flat tire, one unexpected doctor bill, and I wouldn't be able to pay the rent, and I'd have to move back in with my parents.

a date

James graduated from Harvard in journalism and took a job as a reporter for a small newspaper in Alabama. His family was wealthy and lived in New York, but he lived in a ratty apartment and drove a beat-up Chevy with a cracked windshield. I met him when he came to get his teeth cleaned at the dental office where I worked. That weekend we met at a bar for a drink.

James was smart. Really smart. At the bar, we ran into other reporters from the local newspaper and they discussed whether Nixon should be pardoned for the Watergate scandal. I had never been able to figure out what had actually happened with Watergate, so I kept my mouth shut. James didn't seem to mind. When it was time for me to go, he said, "Let's get together next Saturday night. I'll cook."

I spent all day the following Saturday with rollers in my hair. Gave myself a cucumber facial, polished my nails.

That evening, I took Jason to my mother's, where James would pick me up. As soon as he drove into the yard, I went out to meet him so he wouldn't come inside. The outside of my parents' house looked bad enough; I didn't want a *Harvard graduate* to see the shabby furnishings inside.

Surprisingly, James's furniture was far shabbier than anything my mother owned. The faded couch was missing one leg, and his cat had shredded the arms. The stuffing was falling out of the matching chair, and the coffee table was constructed of concrete blocks and a piece of painted plywood. The floor, couch, and table were stacked with the *New York Times,* the local newspaper, and a dozen different magazines. Everything was covered with a thin layer of dust.

"Sorry about the mess," he said, clearing the newspapers from the kitchen table. "I haven't had time to clean."

"That's okay," I said, trying to seem nonchalant. "Can I help you with anything?"

"No, no." He waved me away. "I said I'd cook."

I stood in the middle of the living room, hugging my arms, contemplating the paltry surroundings as James set two places with a napkin, knife, and spoon. He opened two cans of cheese soup and heated it on the battered stove, then poured it into two plastic bowls, broke a loaf of French bread in half, and got out a stick of butter.

He put the food on the table and pulled out my chair. I sat down. He sat next to me and flipped his napkin in the air. Reading my mind, he nodded toward the soup and said, "I want to experience poverty." He gently placed the napkin in his lap.

I stared at him, letting this information settle into my brain. "You can't. You're not poor."

"Yes, but I want the experience of it. That's why I'm living in this dump—to get the *feel* of poverty."

I laughed. "That's absurd. Your family has a million bucks in the bank. Anytime you want to, you can just call home."

"But I won't."

"Doesn't matter. You can't experience poverty if you're not really poor. You've never gone to bed hungry in your entire life."

James took a sip of soup. "That's why I'm eating this stuff."

"Yeah, but you're eating this because you *choose* to eat this—not because you can't afford anything else."

James rolled his shoulders back, irritated with me. I had never associated with anyone like him before, and I didn't want to jeopardize that, so I tried a lighter tone. Half joking, I said, "Personally, I'd like to experience wealth."

James took another sip. "You probably won't."

"Why not?"

"Because you're uneducated."

"I beg your pardon," I said, sitting up straighter. "I'm going to college."

James grimaced. "Yes, well, one class at a time. At night, and at a local college."

"You mean it's not a *Harvard* education." I put down my spoon.

James put his arm around my shoulder. "Don't be offended. I'm merely being *honest*."

I shrugged. "So what do I need to know?" I asked, truly interested.

"Well, let's see." He studied the ceiling for a moment. He leaned back in his chair to get a better look at me. "The classical music that plays in the dental office where you work. Do you know it? Do you know anything about the composers, their music, their lives?"

"A little."

James pulled away from me. "Here, I'll hum a bit and you tell me what it is and who wrote it."

I nodded, dreading the test.

"Pum, pum, pum, puuum," he hummed.

"Beethoven's Fifth," I said.

He smiled broadly. "Very good! I'm impressed."

I blushed and picked up my spoon, hoping he wouldn't continue the test. James started to eat again.

I broke off a piece of bread. "Am I part of your plan to experience poverty?"

James cocked his head as if thinking. "Well, somewhat. I mean, I genuinely *like* you. You've got a certain spark. But I couldn't possibly be in a long-term relationship with you." He waved his spoon at me. "We're from very different worlds, you and I."

I waved my spoon back at him. "That may be, but I'll bet I can get an education more successfully than you can experience poverty."

strike two

*T*hree months after my friend's love affair ended (and the extra $80 a month stopped rolling in), I married Clayton. A Baptist. Built like a bear, he towered over me and made me feel delicate. He owned his own bookbinding business, and though he didn't read books, except for the Bible, which he claimed to have read from cover to cover a number of times, he could bind one to last a lifetime. I married him hoping that some of the kindness he showed to his fellow believers would extend to Jason and me. And it did, as long as I behaved exactly as he wanted me to—and didn't question who was head of the household. I decided I could live with that.

Clayton's soul might have belonged to God, but his worldly possessions were strictly *his*. One afternoon, he and I were standing in the yard when our dog trotted up with a blue velvet box in his mouth. I wrestled it away from him and opened it. Inside was an intricately carved wooden pipe in the shape of a dragon. It was so beautiful that I gasped.

"What is it?" Clayton asked.

I lifted the pipe from the box, examining the bronze bowl and mouthpiece, and held it up for him to take a look.

"Isn't it gorgeous?" I asked.

Clayton stared at it and said, "Throw it away."

"What?" I said, drawing back. "I'm not going to throw it away. I want to make some drawings of it." Already my mind danced with the images of dragons. Since I'd been married to Clayton, my subject matter had been limited. I could draw only objects that he considered *decent:* flowers, birds, mountains.

"It reeks of marijuana," Clayton said. "It's sinful. Throw it away."

I could smell the sweet aroma, but the pipe felt precious, as if it had been a gift. "I'll wash it," I said, and snapped it back into the box.

"You're not taking that pot pipe in my house," Clayton said.

"I'll wash it," I said again. "It's beautiful." I clutched the box tighter as Clayton stepped closer. "Give it to me," he demanded.

"No," I said, and walked toward the house.

Clayton moved in front of me, blocking my way to the steps. "You're not going in *my* house with that pot pipe. Now give it to me."

My cheeks burned hot. "No." Suddenly the pipe didn't matter. I felt that I'd been surrendering to him, rather than to God, and the entity that was *me* had been slipping away. I dropped my head and held the box to my chest. "No," I said again.

Clayton wrapped one huge arm around me and with the other wrenched the box out of my hand. He snapped it open and took the pipe out and dropped it on the concrete step. In one swift move he pushed me aside, picked up a brick, and smashed the pipe to bits. He walked onto the porch and tossed the velvet box as hard as he could into the weeds. "*My* house," he said as he opened the door and went inside.

I should have left a dozen times over, but I couldn't afford to. As the years passed, the transgressions grew. Like the TV evangelists, Clayton had such a special relationship with God that he was exempt from the strict code of moral behavior he imposed on the rest of us. By the time my second marriage ended, I felt so diminished that the spark in my own soul was in mortal danger.

❦

That summer, Jason, who was eight years old, suddenly found his voice. He had opinions on the news, the weather, schoolmates, and of course, me. He came in and stood in the doorway as I wrapped dishes in newspaper. "So where are we going?" he asked.

I couldn't tell if he was disappointed or relieved that we were leaving. "I don't know," I answered.

"Mom, did you know that alligators live in Florida? And sharks?"

"Oh, honey," I said absently, "are you afraid of alligators and sharks?"

"Heck, no," Jason said, shaking the hair from his eyes as if to confront one. "I want to see a real alligator."

"Oh." I *was* afraid of alligators and sharks. And spiders, and the dark, and being alone. I studied Jason for a minute. "What *are* you afraid of?"

He shrugged his shoulders. "Nothing. Bears, maybe. Are there bears in Florida?"

"No, I don't think so." I thought about his answer. Maybe I was afraid of bears too. "Are you afraid of the dark?"

"No," Jason said. "Not as long as you're with me."

I nodded, surprised at the undeserved courage bestowed upon me by this little boy. Lost in my own thoughts, I went back to wrapping dishes.

Jason came over and started putting them into a cardboard box. "Why don't we just move there, Mom? Why don't we just go to Florida?"

For years I'd had a picture of Florida's Ringling School of Art & Design taped to the refrigerator door. Palm trees lined the front of the terra-cotta building, and art students in shorts and straw hats stood sketching the palm trees. I had underlined the address, Sarasota, Florida, in red pencil. For several years in a row, I'd been sending in an application for admittance. Every year an acceptance letter came in the mail, and I'd be elated for days. Even though I couldn't go, I considered my acceptance letters proof that I had talent, that if I had a chance, I could be a *real* artist. Jason thought I was already a real artist.

I stared at him, the set of his jaw, the expectation in his eyes, and realized that I had a responsibility to live up to his assessment of me. I sat down on the floor, light-headed just from the thought of finally following my dream.

When I caught my breath, I called Ringling School of Art & Design to make sure that I could begin classes in the fall, and that financial aid was available.

"Absolutely," the woman in the registrar's office said. "You're set to go."

A few days later Jason and I headed south, driving my beat-up Oldsmobile through Alabama and down the coast of Florida to Sarasota. Home of alligators and sharks, The Ringling Brothers Circus, The John & Mable Ringling Museum, and most important of all, Ringling School of Art & Design. Finally, at twenty-seven, I began chasing the dreams I had conjured when Jason was just a baby.

PART 2

Sarasota, Florida

getting by

*J*ason and I moved into a shabby apartment a few miles from Ringling School of Art & Design. To make ends meet, I took an evening work/study job in the photo lab assisting students with their photo projects.

As a rule, faculty didn't come into the photo lab in the evenings, but one night the photography professor stopped by. The photo lab was set up with a door and then another door made of rubber flaps so the students could come and go from the large darkroom without letting in light that would ruin the film. Red safety lights glowed overhead. When the professor came in, everyone looked up from their work and stopped talking.

"Professor Harris," I said, surprised.

"Well, how are my little cave dwellers tonight?" he asked.

As if on cue, a dozen students said, "Fine," but they didn't go back to work. They stood as if frozen—loops, pliers, and photographs in hand.

Professor Harris frowned. "What?"

Recovering, the students quickly went back to work. One of them said, "Nothing. We're just working away."

Professor Harris took a step backward, and the students cringed in unison. The professor turned and looked behind him. It took a minute for his eyes to adjust to the darkness, to locate the shape the students were staring at. Along the back wall was a dark blue sleeping bag, and someone was wiggling around inside it.

"What in the world?" he asked. He lifted the flap on the bag, and Jason turned over in his sleep, dropping his arm onto the concrete floor.

Professor Harris gasped. "Who's child . . . ?" But he didn't finish the question. He looked right at me and fumbled for his watch. "Why, it's eleven o'clock at night. This child should be at home in bed." Slowly it dawned on him that Jason had been sleeping in the darkroom for months. He glanced down at him, then back at me. "Is that sleeping bag thick enough? That concrete's awfully cold. Maybe we should put a blanket underneath it." He was quiet for a moment, rubbing his jaw. Then he said, "For Christ sakes, it's eleven o'clock at night. All of you get out. It's closing time."

Since leaving Alabama, keeping Jason safe had been my biggest concern. In Sarasota, the duplex apartment we had moved into was in a poor neighborhood. Crack addicts wandered the streets, looking for something worth stealing, something easy to resell. There was no way I could leave my son alone in their midst. Right off the bat, my next-door neighbor, Charlene, offered to keep an eye on him for just a few dollars, paid in advance. Relieved, I gave her $5, and went to the photo lab. When I got in from work that night, Charlene wasn't home. I found her at the gas station, pumping quarters into a black-jack machine. Jason was asleep in a chair by the door. Anyone could have taken him and Charlene wouldn't have noticed until she ran out of quarters.

That's how Jason wound up sleeping in the darkroom, where I could see him, where I knew he was safe. Fortunately Professor Harris seemed to understand all this and never said a word about it.

On Saturday mornings, I painted designs on surfboards for a local surfboard company. Cash. No questions asked. Jason was my assistant. We'd go early and throw open the garage-style door of the huge metal building so it could air out. Even at dawn, it was stifling inside. No air-conditioning. No ventilation. We went at daybreak to beat the hot Florida sun and the accumulation of fumes.

My art supplies—water-based paints, brushes, charcoal pencils, and colored chalks—were stashed in an old Western Flyer red wagon for easy handling. Jason pulled the wagon along behind me, handing me whatever I asked for. I painted quick, free-flowing designs that appealed to teenagers.

"Yellow," I piped, like a doctor standing over a surgical field. Jason handed me the paint. With his help, I could knock out 120 surfboards in three hours. At a dollar a board, that was 120 tax-free dollars.

But it wasn't enough to keep us afloat. When we got desperate, we'd walk the streets looking for soda bottles and beer cans to sell back to the grocery store for the deposit money. One day as we walked along the alley looking for cans, Jason said, "Mom, I'm going to babysit."

"For who?" I asked.

"Maria, across the street."

Maria worked the graveyard shift at the International House of Pancakes. Even pregnant, she could load six piping-hot plates on her arms at one time. A month ago, she left work to have her baby. She had been home ever since. She didn't have a husband or a boyfriend, and her parents lived in Germany. I had no idea how she had been surviving for the past month.

"That'll be nice," I said. "When I was a teenager, I babysat almost every Saturday night. I made pretty good money too."

"Not Saturday night," Jason said. "Every night."

I looked at my son.

"She's going back to work on Monday," Jason said, "and I'm going to keep Benjamin all night for ten dollars a night. She gets off work at seven in the morning, and the school bus doesn't come until seven-thirty."

"What?"

"Ten dollars a night," Jason said.

I felt my jaw drop as I calculated in my head. *Maria works five nights a week. Four weeks in a month.*

"That's two hundred dollars a month," I said incredulously.

"Yeah," Jason said. "If you'll help me, I'll split it with you."

I laughed out loud. Benjamin was four weeks old. Maria knew when she asked Jason to babysit that she was really asking me.

The houses in our neighborhood were so close together they

practically touched. The street was narrow, and our block was a dead end, which meant almost no traffic. From my living room, I could see through the open jalousie windows on Maria's front door into her kitchen. Maria was German; her dishes were red German willow, and on top of her refrigerator sat a dozen hand-painted beer steins with music-box bases. In the evenings she'd wind them, one at a time, and sit on her front steps while they wound down. Brahms, Strauss, Liszt, Bach, Wagner.

I knew her work schedule. Knew when a lover stayed over, when there was a fight. Knew when the lack of air-conditioning made her move at a slower pace. Yet I wouldn't necessarily think to say we were friends. Maria spoke very little English, just enough to get by, so we didn't have long conversations when we occasionally stood in the street and talked.

Still, after the initial shock, I wasn't surprised that she had asked Jason to watch Benjamin. Just as I knew about her life, she knew about mine. She had seen me sitting at the kitchen table helping Jason with his homework and watched me shoot hoops with him in the yard. Day after day, she'd heard me yell, praise, and soothe.

We had just gotten home from the photo lab one night when Maria dashed over and handed a sleeping newborn to a sleepy nine-year-old. She tossed the diaper bag onto the sofa and waved as she ran out the door. *"Danke,"* she said. "Thank you." Jason yawned and stumbled off to bed, tucking Benjamin under the covers beside him as if he were a teddy bear.

this time

*D*ewy lived in the garage apartment behind the house on the corner. He worked as a waiter. Since the day Jason and I met him, he'd been fired four times. Like a number of young men in the neighborhood, he was addicted to crack cocaine. And like the others, when he was off work, or out of work, he played basketball in the warm Florida sunshine. I had had no idea that a basketball hoop in the driveway would attract a barrage of junkies. I had it installed right after we moved in, knowing it would make Jason happy, and that it would keep him in his own yard—where I could keep an eye on him. But the dopers came in twos and threes, shirtless and clammy, pink-eyed and sniffling, to play one-on-one, H-O-R-S-E, or just to stand, vacantly, and shoot the basketball shot after shot into the net.

At first, I was terrified of them, and angry because I didn't think Jason should be playing basketball with drug addicts. But little by little Dewy won me over.

He stood in my doorway, wearing gym shorts and tennis shoes, chest puffed out, looking right into my eyes. "I'd never let anything happen to Jason," he said, holding up his right hand as if to make a pledge. "I just got out of rehab. I'm done with drugs. I'm gonna go to school." He turned and waved his arm as if presenting a view of our neighborhood. "I'm gonna go to school and be a counselor so I can help those poor bastards that are hooked like I used to be." He looked down. "I can do it this time." He paused, then looked at me again. "Really. I'm gonna make it this time."

I let Jason shoot hoops with him, but I watched through the open windows, listening to every word they said. Mostly they talked about layups, rebounds, and free throws. "Air ball!" they cried, when the basketball missed the net altogether.

Days went by and Dewy seemed to be doing all right. Then one day he could hardly play. His hands shook so badly he couldn't make a single basket. He stopped on the sideline to catch his breath, the basketball tucked under his armpit. He wiped his nose on the back of his hand. "Jason, don't never let nobody talk you into doing drugs," he said. "It'll eat you up. Eat your life."

Jason nodded and started to run back onto the court, but Dewy didn't move. "No, man, I'm serious. Don't try it. Not even once. I been in rehab three times, and I can't shake it." Dewy held the ball out on his hand. It shook in his palm for a few seconds then fell to the ground. "I can't even hold a basketball—and I used to be pretty good."

The next day Dewy came to the door to ask if Jason could shoot some hoops. His eyes blazed. Sweat trickled down his forehead.

"For just a few minutes," I said, glancing at Jason, who was behind me, staring at Dewy with a disappointed expression on his face. "He's got homework." I went outside too and pretended to prune the small lime tree that was growing beside the house. I snipped a limb from the top and picked a few dead leaves from the branches.

Dewy and Jason ran across the parking lot. The basketball slammed into the backboard. They ran again. I could hear the air forced in and out of Dewy's lungs. Suddenly he stopped short and reeled. I dropped the pruning scissors and watched him move in a slow circle.

"Dewy?" Jason said.

Dewy fell to the pavement and began twitching and jerking.

"Mom!" Jason cried. I ran over and pushed Jason toward the house. "Go call 911." I tried to hold Dewy down, but he was stronger than I was. He bit his tongue and blood ran into the foam that bubbled around his mouth and nose. The convulsions got more violent. He pitched back and forth, his arms curled into his chest. The pavement scraped his forehead, nose, elbows, and knees. I ran inside and got some towels, but his spasms knocked them away. I squatted and held his legs down so his face wouldn't hit the pavement anymore. Blood and saliva flew everywhere. I dropped my head to protect my face. A long minute later, the jerking eased to mild tremors. I put a towel under Dewy's head and wiped the blood and spit from his mouth with another. Jason came back and squatted beside me. He buried his face in my shoulder. "Do something," he whispered.

"There's nothing I can do," I said.

By the time the ambulance got there, the seizure was over. Dewy was unconscious and looked as if he'd been beaten half to death.

That evening Dewy was back home. I stood on the front porch and watched him walk toward our house, slightly stooped, weary, eyes bloodshot from the seizure. He sat on the porch beside Jason and picked at the black, crusty scab on his knee.

"Sorry I scared you, man," he said.

"That's okay," Jason said. "You all right?"

"Yeah." Dewy sat up straight and rolled his shoulders back. "Well, not really. It's the drugs, you know."

Jason nodded.

Dewy wiped his nose with the hem of his T-shirt. "I don't reckon I'll ever be all right." He sucked in his breath and let it out slowly. "I thought I was gonna make it this time."

They sat quietly for a moment. Then Jason nudged Dewy's shoulder with his. He grabbed the basketball and jumped to his feet. "Come on, man," he said, dribbling the ball toward the court. "That was just a minor setback. You'll be able to do it this time."

Dewy put his elbows on his knees and hung his head. He let out a quick, cynical laugh and said, "Yeah," then climbed off the step and shuffled onto the court.

Alabama
kicking at the moon

*H*omesick, Jason and I drove to Alabama for a visit. Jason stayed with Clayton, and I stayed with Mother. Every fall, my sister Doris Ann throws a barbecue, and I was excited to go.

By the time my baby sister, Janet, now seventeen, and I arrived, several guys had already pulled out their guitars and set up a band out in a dirt-patch, pine-shaded area. They were playing "Bad, Bad, Leroy Brown," and I could tell by the rhythm, or lack of it, that at least half of them were well on their way to drunk. A group of women I'd never seen before sat in lawn chairs, beer in hand, singing out of tune. A few couples wandered aimlessly through the pine grove under the full moon—the second one in that month, a blue moon. Half-naked kids ran in and out of the neighboring houses, and up and down the steep, path-beaten yard.

Stewart and John played guitar with the band, and my brother Willie watched them, as Doris Ann tried to light the bonfire pyramid she'd built of old lumber, tree limbs, Coke crates, and broken chairs. She'd bought a Doberman, Mickey, after her house was broken into, and he was now maniacally barking and running back and forth inside the chain-link fence.

"This damned fire!" Doris Ann yelled. "I've been trying to get it going for half an hour." She threw the matches on the ground, slammed through the chain-link fence to the house, and came back with a can of lighter fluid. She squirted the lighter fluid onto the pile, soaking several pieces of lumber and part of a chair.

"Never plan a goddamned party with drunk idiots," she said. "I've been working all day to get this place in shape." She tossed her long sandy hair over her shoulder, then waved a hand toward the group of people down by the music. "Nobody else has done a thing! Everybody's too drunk to cook, and I'm not standing here all night cooking for thirty people." She reached for the matches. Instinctively the three of us backed up as she struck a match and tossed it onto the heap. Instantly she had a bonfire the size of a bed, and several neighbor kids ran toward the blaze.

Doris Ann pointed at them, and they stopped short. "Get on back down the hill," she said. "The bonfire is for adults only." The fire leapt ten feet into the air and climbed up two pine trees at the corner of her yard, catching the lower limbs ablaze. Flames shot up into the sky. From where I stood, it looked as if she'd caught the moon on fire.

Doris Ann threw a look at Janet and me. "Don't say a word."

I grinned. "I wasn't going to."

Janet cocked her head and stared at the blaze. "Me neither."

Doris Ann slammed back through the fence and grabbed the garden hose, but it wouldn't reach the fire. She jerked the hose out as far as it would go but it still wouldn't reach. She soaked the trunks of each tree, occasionally glancing down the hill to see if any of the guys had even noticed. They happily strummed their guitars and continued drinking.

"I don't like those pine trees that close to my yard anyway. I hope they burn to the ground." She squirted a ring around the bonfire to keep it contained and tossed the hose aside. Inside the wet circle, the fire roared like an angry storm and spit bits of fire into the air. I was afraid the intense heat or a spark might fly over and blow up one of the pickup trucks parked randomly in the driveway, so I moved farther away, watching the heat shimmer over the moon and distort the perfectly round shape of it.

🌿

An hour later, the fire had burned down to a huge pile of smoldering red coals. The golden moon had climbed high in the sky. Stewart put down his guitar, grabbed another beer, and came over to the fire, where Doris Ann, Janet, and I stood warming our hands and staring up at the sky. Stewart was completely intoxicated, and in a good mood. He smiled at me as he weaved back and forth in front of the hot coals. "You still in school, Barbara?" he asked.

"Yeah."

Stewart laughed and, teasing, asked, "Ain't you learned nothing yet?"

"Not much," I admitted. "I figure if I haven't learned anything by the time I'm forty, I'll give it up."

Stewart laughed again. He looked at Janet. "Damn, Janet. I can't believe you're a grown woman. I still think of you as little bitty." He put his arm around her and she buried her face in his chest.

Willie came up and held his palms toward the hot coals. He'd been drinking but he wasn't as drunk as the others. He said, "Do you know why I'm not a famous trumpet player like Al Hirt?"

I smiled and said, "No."

"Procrastination. Procrastination, procrastination, procrastination. I intended to practice but I procrastinated, and then one day I was old."

Even though I knew he was serious, I laughed out loud. "Well, you had a beat-up old trumpet."

Willie shook his head and interrupted, "No. I procrastinated. A beat-up trumpet still plays. If I had worked at it, I could have been good."

Stewart held up his beer and said, "That's right. A beat-up trumpet still plays."

I nodded, but being a year ahead of Willie in school, I remembered how cruel the other band members had been about his old, dented trumpet. And I remembered the day that the kids at school had circled around him, taunting, laughing, kicking at him, until he couldn't take it anymore and came home and tossed that battered trumpet into the closet, closing the door on it forever.

Just then, a rusty white van roared up the driveway. Two young men with dishwater-blond hair climbed out and staggered over to the fire. Strangers. Inside the fence, Mickey, the Doberman, crouched low, bared his teeth, and growled. The men peered into the fire with blazing red eyes, held their hands out, and rubbed them together. They reeked of whiskey, pot, and body odor. One of them was wearing a white T-shirt with a Dixie flag on the front. The arms of the shirt had been cut out all the way to the waist, and his flabby waistline sagged out the sides. The other one, a little taller and thinner, had on a black T-shirt with a hooded figure on the front. It read, *It's a white thing. You wouldn't understand.* The man wearing the Dixie flag turned to Stewart and said, "We're here to recruit for the Aryan nation. The numbers are getting low, and we need some new men."

Stewart chuckled. "I thought the Aryans were suppose to be of superior intelligence. You dumb sons-a-bitches couldn't pour piss out of a boot if the directions was on the bottom."

Doris Ann and I froze. Janet made a weak noise like a newborn kitten. I reached out and pulled on her sleeve. "Let's go," I whispered. She started to back away but in an instant recovered and put her arm around my waist, stopping me. "Just a minute," she said. "They don't have guns."

"Stewart," I cried, "move away from the fire." Stewart ignored me.

Dixie flag pointed to Stewart. "I'll fuckin' shoot you." He took off for the van, and his sidekick followed him.

Stewart yelled, "Good!"

John heard the commotion, put down his guitar, and walked over, assessing the situation.

Dixie flag threw open the side door of the van and pulled out a pistol. He steadied himself and tried to stuff bullets in the chamber, but his hands trembled and he dropped them. As he picked them up, he mumbled, "I'm gonna fuckin' blow you to pieces."

Black T-shirt leaned against the driver's side door and watched his partner. He reached down to help pick up the bullets but his partner kicked at him.

Us girls backed against Doris Ann's fence, but Mickey snarled and bashed against it from the other side, sending us back toward the fire.

Stewart hadn't moved. He chuckled as he watched the two men try to load the pistol.

John, who was the only sober man for half a mile, casually walked up to the van and asked, "What can I do for you two?"

"I'm gonna shoot that son of a bitch right there," Dixie flag said, pointing the gun at Stewart. John looked at the gun, then looked over his shoulder at Stewart, then back to the gun.

"Not with that pistol, you're not. Those bullets don't go to that gun."

Dixie flag blinked and tried to focus on the gun in his hand. "Goddamnit!" he said, and tossed it into the van. It clattered against empty beer cans, and the cans rolled out onto the red dirt.

"Well, I'm gonna go get some bullets that do fit, and I'm gonna come back and kill that traitor son of a bitch right there," he yelled.

Stewart laughed and tipped back his beer.

John pulled a shiny, new Luger from the small of his back and held it toward the night sky. Jolted to life, the two men scrambled into the side door of the van and slammed it shut. They climbed into the seats up front, and Dixie flag quickly started the engine.

John held the pistol as if he were born with it in his hand. He said, "You can go, but I'd think twice about coming back."

Dixie flag threw the van into gear and backed all the way down the driveway. He slammed into a small pine tree at the bottom of the hill, drove forward, and scraped it again as he backed onto the road. Dixie flag and Black T-shirt hung out the windows. "We'll get you!" they shouted. "We'll be back to kill you all!"

John tucked the Luger back into his belt and kicked hot coals farther into the fire. "You gonna play, Stewart?" he asked.

Stewart tossed his beer can against the fence and, copying John, kicked a tuft of red dirt into the molten coals. Dusting his hands on his jeans, he said, "Yeah. Let's go." The boys headed down the hill to their guitars. Shot with adrenaline, us girls walked back to the fire. We stood there for a minute, lost in our thoughts. I could see the reflection of the moon in the smoldering flames. Finally we looked at each other. Doris Ann rolled her eyes.

I said, "I'm getting out of here before they get back."

"Me too," Janet said, knowing I wouldn't let her stay.

Doris Ann shrugged her shoulders and with conviction said, "They ain't coming back." She picked up a pinecone and tossed it into the fire.

dating

*P*hillip lived in a large stucco house with a Spanish-tiled roof a couple of blocks from my apartment in Sarasota. I met him while I was combing the neighborhood for beer cans and pop bottles to sell back to the store for the deposit. He thought I was out for a walk. I took an alternative route home so he didn't see me with my armload of dirty bottles. About the third time I walked down his street, he struck up a conversation, and before I walked on, he had asked me if I'd like to go to dinner.

The following Friday, one of my girlfriends watched Jason, and I went out on a date. Phillip took me to a posh restaurant on Lido Square, the ritzy tourist trap down by the beach. The tables had crocheted tablecloths, fresh-cut orchids in crystal vases, and candles.

"What kind of wine do you like?" he asked as we studied the menu. I didn't have any idea. I said, "I'll trust your judgment." The waiter came and Phillip ordered a pinot noir. I scanned the wine list for the label. One hundred dollars a bottle! I smiled at Phillip and said, "Nice." I felt mildly ill. Jason and I could eat for two months on $100. I held the menu in front of me. The entrées were listed without prices. I gazed over the top and studied Phillip: starched white shirt, blue tie, black slacks, slicked-back hair.

Phillip closed his menu and put it aside. "So, you're in art school?"

"Yes." I put the menu down.

Phillip nodded. "That's great." He paused. "What do you plan to do once you get out of school? I mean"—he put his hands flat on the table—"how do you plan to make a living."

Before I could answer, the waiter came again. Relieved, I turned my attention to the task at hand, but could feel the weight of the question hanging in the air. Phillip was a single investment broker; he helped people make intelligent financial decisions. I was a broke, single mother. My financial decisions were simple: Do I buy shampoo this month or wash my hair with diluted dishwashing liquid?

Phillip ordered steak and I ordered fried jumbo shrimp. I handed the menu back to the waiter and looked at Phillip. "I plan to teach art history at the college level," I lied. "Art defines a culture, don't you think?"

He raised his eyebrows. "That's great. College professors make a decent living." Then his brow furrowed. "Personally, I don't see the point in art. I mean, I like some of it." He snapped his fingers several times, thinking. "Michelangelo. He painted the Sistine Chapel, right?"

I nodded.

"But he didn't make any money," he said. "And he was as good as it gets."

"Yes, but—"

"Now, come on," Phillip said, sitting back in his chair. "He was as good as it gets."

I tried to redirect the conversation. For several years I'd been studying the financial pages in the newspaper. I knew the tickers for dozens of blue-chip stocks—and thought he'd find that impressive. "Tell me about investing," I said. "I've always been interested in the stock market. I'd like to build a portfolio someday."

"That's good. But you need to come to your senses about the art world or you'll never make enough money to invest in anything."

I smiled. Nodded. Kept quiet.

Our dinners arrived. "Art school doesn't make any sense to me," he said. "Why would you pay money to get an education in something you can't make a living doing?"

I tried to keep the disappointment from showing on my face.

After all, he was just being honest—which was more than I'd been. I hadn't told him about my real plans for the future—that all I really wanted to do was make art. And I hadn't mentioned Jason at all. He didn't know I had a child waiting for me to come home.

With that thought in mind, I studied the table, picking out treats for him. I had brought my black purse with a zip closure. Inside the coin case, I'd stashed a few quarters and dimes—in case I needed to make a phone call—and a lipstick. The rest of it was empty, except for several ziplock plastic bags.

While Phillip cut his steak and denounced art school, I ate my baked potato and steamed vegetables and furtively slipped the shrimp from my plate into a plastic bag in my purse.

"Are you going to drink this?" he asked, gesturing toward my glass of wine. He'd already emptied the bottle.

"Go ahead."

While Phillip drank my wine, I quietly emptied the remaining dinner rolls and sweet breads from the bread basket, along with several pats of butter.

"And we should get rid of the National Endowment for the Arts," he said, putting my empty glass back in front of my plate. He wiped his mouth on his napkin. "The guy pissed in a bucket and dropped a crucifix in it. That's not art! And my taxes are paying for that crap."

The couple at the next table glared at us, and I wiggled uncomfortably in my seat. "Yes, I see your point." I spotted the silver sugar bowl. Jason had never seen sugar served in little pink cubes. (Neither had I for that matter.) I dropped a half dozen into my bag.

Phillip ordered dessert for both of us: a cup of coffee, and hazelnut ice cream, which I'd never had before, served with chocolate biscotti. I ate the ice cream and, while Phillip tallied the bill, discreetly tucked the cookies into my purse. Just for good measure, I threw in the fancy paper doily from under my coffee cup.

tumbler music

*I*n the middle of the night, our neighbor Charlene moved out of her half of our duplex. We discovered she was gone when her cat—abandoned inside the apartment—began to wail. Jason peeked through the window. "Her furniture's gone." He tried the front door. "She owed her bookie money. She borrowed a thousand dollars from him and lost it at the horse track."

"Her bookie?" I asked, slipping my student ID into the crack of the door, trying to release the latch. It wouldn't budge. The cat scratched the floor on the other side. "Poor baby."

We tried the back door and the windows. The place was locked tight. Charlene wasn't mean-spirited. The cat must accidentally have been locked inside when she left.

Jason picked up a brick. "We can't leave that cat in there. We've got to break in." I followed him around to the side of the house, surveying the neighborhood to make sure no one was watching us. I snapped the window screen loose and dropped it on the ground. "Let me do it," I said, taking the brick. I tapped the glass until it cracked, then tapped it some more until the pieces fell to the floor inside the apartment. I looked around again to make sure nobody had heard the breaking glass. I rubbed the brick along the window frame, clearing the remaining shards from the wood, then tossed the brick aside. I leaned into the room. It was much bigger than the bedroom in our apartment.

"I'll go," Jason said, effortlessly swinging himself through the window.

By the time I ran around the house, Jason had scooped up the cat and opened the back door. "It stinks in here," he said.

Charlene must have left in a hurry. Dirty dishes filled the sink, trash tumbled from the cabinet underneath. The floor was cluttered with clothes, soup cans, pizza boxes, beer bottles, and shoes. The cat had been using the pizza boxes as litterboxes, and from the mess, we realized Charlene had been gone longer than we thought. I walked through the house, opening doors and windows to let in some air. Jason dropped the cat and he scampered onto the screened-in back porch.

"This place is great," Jason said. "*Two* bedrooms." He thumped the refrigerator door. "Look at this, Mom."

A fairly new refrigerator. When Jason and I had moved into our apartment, it didn't even have a refrigerator. We used a red plastic Igloo cooler for five months before the property management company brought the battered clunker we were presently using. They promised a newer one, along with a stove that worked, but we never heard from them again.

I walked into the bathroom. Several pairs of flowered panties hung along the edge of a claw-foot tub. I thought of relaxing in that warm tub instead of standing in our closet-size shower.

"Let's move in here," I said.

Jason came and stood in the doorway. "Can we afford it?"

The rent for Charlene's apartment was $150 more a month than ours. I shrugged. "The property management company hasn't been out here in a year. If we don't tell them, they'll never know."

Jason looked at me, his jaw dropping. "What if they catch us?"

I considered this. "I guess they could evict us. That's about the worst that could happen. But I don't think they'll even notice. When was the last time someone came out here?"

Jason looked at the floor.

"They're supposed to cut the grass every month; I have to pay a fee for it—but they never do it. They didn't even come out last year when that hurricane blew down half the trees in the neighborhood. Remember? We called them a dozen times, then cleaned up the mess ourselves."

Jason nodded. We stood, transfixed, lost in our thoughts.

"Okay," Jason said. "Let's move in."

In a rush of adrenaline, we ran through the apartment collecting Charlene's junk and tossing it onto the back porch. We laughed, giddy with excitement. We cleaned all day. At dusk, we loaded the trash and junk into garbage bags and dragged them to the green Dumpster behind the Dairy Queen on the corner. The next day we replaced the broken window and moved in our belongings, one piece at a time. I called a locksmith and told him I'd lost my keys. He took the locks apart and spent an hour fitting new keys. Tumbler music, that faint sound of opening, filled the apartment. While the locksmith worked, Jason painted the mailboxes that hung between the front doors of the apartments. When they dried, I painted new black letters on the front of each box, switching the apartment numbers.

I was standing on the front porch when the mailman came the next day. He hesitated only briefly before dropping my mail into the new mailbox. He lifted his eyebrows and walked on.

at this late date

Out of the blue, without any warning, Rudy, my ex-husband and Jason's biological father, called me in Florida saying he wanted to be in Jason's life.

"When will you be coming home?" he asked. "I want to spend some time with my son."

It irked me, the way he said *my son*, as if he saw him all the time, as if he hadn't been completely absent from his son's life for twelve years. And why now? Why did he suddenly want to see Jason? It didn't take me long to worm it out of him.

"I got remarried," he said. "I've got a stepson Jason's age."

Rudy still lived in my hometown, Anniston, Alabama. And I happened to know that he'd been married and divorced several times since we'd been together. But to my knowledge, Jason was his only child. Acquiring a stepson must have triggered this newfound interest in fatherhood.

Still, I was leery—and told him I'd have to think about it. That old fear that he'd kidnap Jason still triggered a rush of adrenaline. Jason was too big, too smart, for that to be a real danger anymore, but that didn't eliminate those years of worry and the anger. When Jason was little, I had been so afraid he'd be snatched away from me that I'd stood guard outside the doors of public rest rooms and dressing rooms, wouldn't let him go alone to the concession stand at the movies, kept him from riding his bicycle around the block. I had hated this man for making me so afraid. But now, I simply felt sorry for him. He had missed it. First words, first grade, first kiss. Missed it all.

But that little boy was now taller than I was. What did *he* want?

Jason was standing in the yard tossing the basketball into the hoop when I told him Rudy wanted to see him. He held the basketball over his head for a second, then lowered it. "Why?" he asked.

"He wants to get to know you?"

Jason tucked the ball under his arm and faced me, shifting his weight onto one foot. "Why?" he asked again. He didn't say it with malice, but with genuine curiosity. Rudy's new stepson came to mind but I didn't mention him. I studied my child, recognizing his father's square jaw and sinewy muscles. Finally I gave him the only answer I could come up with: "I don't know."

Jason stared at the ground for a minute. Then he shrugged and tossed the ball into the hoop. "I guess it's fine."

Every year Jason and I drove to Alabama to spend the Christmas holidays with Mother. When Rudy called back, I told him to meet us at her house.

"That's great," he said. "I'll take him out to the strip pits for some target practice."

The passing of time and the distance made me brave. "No. I've kept him away from guns. Besides, the people that go out to the strip pits are careless. Half of them are drunk. It's not safe."

I could feel Rudy's annoyance through the receiver. He wasn't used to me calling the shots. He started to protest, but quickly changed his mind.

"Fine," he said. "I'll take him to the arcade."

Mother didn't approve of Jason going anywhere with Rudy. "I don't think he deserves to spend time with my grandbaby," she said. We'd gotten to her house the night before, and she said this to me as soon as Jason went to bed. She said it again the next morning, and again.

"Besides, I want him to help decorate the Christmas tree," she said. "He loves to hang the lights."

My sister Janet had stacked the decorations in the living room. She sat on the floor, opening the boxes. "You made these, Barbara," she said, holding up a salt clay angel. "When I was about seven years old. Remember?"

"I remember," I said, smiling. Janet was so much younger than the rest of us, in a sense, like Jason, she had been an only child. And like Jason, her father had somewhat abandoned her too. Mother and Dad had gotten a divorce when she was a little girl. Since then, she seldom heard from him. Janet was a college student, but occasionally she and Jason would band together like long-lost siblings and discuss school activities, rap music—and occasionally, the absence of a father in their lives.

I sat down beside Janet and picked out a decoration to admire. "We can wait until this afternoon to decorate the tree, Mom," I said.

Mother stared at the bare cedar tree in the red tree stand in front of the window.

I dropped the decoration back in the box. "I don't know what else to do," I said. "You know how mean he can be. If I tell him he can't see Jason, there's no telling what he'll do."

Mother looked at me and said, "Which is exactly why I don't want him around my grandbaby."

Rudy drove into the yard and we all ran to the window to see what he was driving. A black Thunderbird with yellow racing stripes.

"That's just what I would have guessed," Mother said.

Janet and I laughed. Jason had been in the bedroom getting dressed. He ran into the living room, buttoning his shirt, and peeked over my shoulder. "Is that him?"

I nodded. Rudy and his stepson climbed out of the car. Rudy looked older, but remarkably the same. He was tall, blond, and hand-some. A twinge of loss ran through me. I had needed this man, and he hadn't noticed. I had loved him, and he hadn't cared. I inhaled a deep breath and slowly released it. I smiled as Rudy walked toward the house. Jason walked just like that, a long, casual gait with a slight lilt to the right. As he approached the front door, we jumped away from the window and scattered around the room, trying to look normal.

He knocked. Mother feigned interest in the tree lights, letting me know that she would have no part in this. I opened the door. Rudy stepped back. "Well, hi," he said as his eyes swept over me. He pushed the boy ahead of him into the living room and acknowledged Janet and Mother with a nod and a smile. When he got to Jason, he stopped short and his eyes widened. He backed up slightly, then cocked his head. "Jason?"

Jason shook his head and stuck out his hand.

Rudy was completely taken aback. "I can't believe it." Apparently he had lost track of the years. In his mind, Jason was the same age as the seven-year-old boy clinging to his side. It took several seconds for him to recover his poise. He took Jason's hand and shook it, examining him from head to toe. Instead of just letting go, he pulled him close and hugged him, patting his back. "Well, Jason, you're soon gonna be as tall as your old man." He held him out and looked at him. "My goodness. You're practically grown!" He cleared his throat again. "I can't believe it." He looked over at me. "You did a fine job, Barbara."

I smiled, surprised that he'd give me any credit. "Thank you," I said.

The little boy buried his face in Rudy's shirt. Rudy caught him by the shoulders and eased him in front of us. "This is my stepson, Robert."

"Hi, Robert," we chimed.

The little boy whispered, "Hi," and studied his feet.

We fell silent. Nobody seemed to know what to say next. Rudy fidgeted, then, in an exaggerated gesture, threw up his hands and said, "Well, Son, let's go to the arcade."

Jason looked at me expectantly. "Okay," he said.

"It's cold outside," Rudy said. "Get your coat."

Jason walked over and picked up his coat from the couch. "Get your coat, Mom," he said.

Surprised, I opened my mouth to protest, but Rudy cut me off. "She's not going."

Jason looked at me with a shocked expression on his face. I realized that he had assumed I was going too. He hugged his jacket to his chest and eyed Rudy suspiciously. "I'm not going if she doesn't go."

Startled, everyone looked at Jason. Rudy stepped toward him. "Son," he said, gesturing with his hands again, "I want to spend some time with *you*."

"That's fine," Jason said, nodding, "but if she doesn't go, I'm not going."

My jaw dropped. Half recovering, I said, "It's all right, Jason. You'll be fine."

Rudy said, "Just you and me."

Jason straightened and addressed Rudy in a tone of voice I'd never heard before, a man's voice. "I don't know you, and I'm not going anywhere with you unless she goes with me."

There was a stunned silence in the room.

Rudy blushed. He tried to laugh but it came out choked. He shifted his weight from one foot to the other, and back again. Then his face darkened and his lips drew tight. He pointed at me. "You did this," he shouted. "You turned my son against me! You fuckin' turned my son against me!"

My mouth fell open. Through the years, I'd never said an unkind word to Jason about his father. Secretly, I'd always hoped that Rudy would someday want to get to know his son. At this late date, it would take some time—but it could still be accomplished.

Apparently Rudy didn't have that kind of time. He grabbed Robert and shoved him out the front door, slamming it as hard as he could. Rudy kicked a flowerpot off the steps and we heard it break into pieces. We all ran to the window again. They climbed into the Thunderbird. Red-faced and angry, Rudy cranked the car, spun it around, and floored it, flinging dirt and gravel everywhere. The Thunderbird sped down the road and disappeared.

We moved away from the window as if in a trance. I walked over to Jason and leaned my shoulder into his. He smiled faintly.

Janet said, "Shoot." She and Jason exchanged disappointed looks.

"Yeah," he said.

Mother walked over and picked up the Christmas tree lights. "Well," she said, handing the bundle to Jason, "we might as well decorate this tree." She popped the plug into the wall. The string of lights flickered, then snapped to life.

dating

I met Lewis at the photo lab. He too was an art student at Ringling, his last year. But his grades were low and he didn't get along with his teachers. He would come into the photo lab the night before an assignment was due and insist that I keep the lab open until he finished his work. At some point I started helping him so I could get home.

"I'm better than everyone in my class," Lewis said, lifting a photograph of a palm tree out of the developing tray. "But the teachers give me bad grades because I turn my work in late. And they think it's late because I smoke too much reefer. But they're wrong. I do my best work smoked up." He handed the photo to me, and I pinned it up to dry. "You and me, we're going out this weekend."

It wasn't a question; it was a command. I didn't know how to get out of it without making him angry. And I'd seen him angry. When he didn't get his way, he smashed things. Still, I didn't worry about it too much. Lewis would be graduating in a few weeks and had already lined up a job in Chicago.

I attended Lewis's graduation with a sigh of relief. Secretly I had been marking off the days until he would leave for Chicago. Nothing I did pleased him. He was jealous of the relationship I had with my teachers, jealous of my artwork, my grades—even jealous of my son. Reminiscent of my ex-husbands (both of them), he kept track of my every move. He even followed me to church a couple of times. I was sick to death of him—but too scared to break off the relationship. I had attempted it in the past with disastrous results.

"I'll kill myself," he had said. "And I'll kill you."

For me, his departure for Chicago shined in the future like a bright star.

✿

A couple of weeks after his graduation, Lewis slammed through my door without knocking and raked everything off the kitchen table onto the floor. "Those son of a bitches!" he shouted. "They hired somebody else!"

My heart felt like it dropped to my toes. "Why?"

Lewis swiped a stack of old mail off the counter. "They claim I never sent my résumé! Hell, I talked to them on the phone five times. They said I was the man for the job. You took forever with that goddamn résumé, Barbara!"

I felt sick and sat down in the rocking chair, my mind racing. He was insinuating that this was my fault. I had edited his résumé, but had given it back to him weeks ago and told him to send it. Apparently he never did.

He walked around the apartment with his hands in his pockets, stopping in front of me. In a calm voice he said, "I guess I'll look for a job here."

It occurred to me then that he hadn't sent the résumé on purpose. Without telling me, his plans had changed—and his new plans included me. I locked my arms across my chest and instinctively my body began to gently rock back and forth.

peashooter

My brother John joined the military right out of high school and stayed in. He had recently reenlisted for another tour and had been given thirty days' leave to goof off before he had to report back to duty. He called to let me know he would be showing up at my house the following Saturday.

"Sergeant Moss, reporting for duty," he said when he arrived, swinging his duffel bag over his shoulder, and playfully snapping a salute.

I threw my arms around him. "I'm so glad you're here," I said, and ran my hand over his bristle-cut brown hair. His hair was short and straight, mine was long and curly; other than that, we looked incredibly alike. We were thin and wiry, and the same wrinkle pattern had started to web around our eyes.

"Where's Jason?" John asked.

"He's at a friend's house. We'll go get him in a few minutes."

John looked around the apartment, noticed the windows, then glanced at the door again. "Why is there steel on the door and windows?"

I shrugged. "I bolted it on there so nobody could break in."

John laced his fingers through the mesh on the door and shook it. "You couldn't break through that with a bazooka." He studied me then. "Is the neighborhood that bad?"

I rubbed my arms as if warming myself, thinking about the hooker who had lived in the other duplex apartment for a couple of months.

Her clients had traipsed in and out all hours of the night. "Yes," I said, and then, "No." I sighed. "It's just that the crack addicts wander around this area, and . . . well, my ex-boyfriend has been stalking me. He tried to break in the door, and he smashed out the windows in my bedroom one night, so I covered all the openings with expanded steel."

John dropped his duffel bag onto the floor. "I need to have a little talk with this guy."

"No," I said, waving off John's remark, "everything's fine now."

He glared at me. "You don't bolt steel to your door when everything's fine." We stood there silently as if in a trance for a minute, then he went out to his pickup truck and dug around behind the seat. He pulled out a pistol and came back inside. He took my hand and smacked the pistol into my palm, a Smith & Wesson .22. "Just in case," he said.

As we were growing up, Dad had taught all of us kids to shoot a rifle. I was a pretty good shot—with a rifle. But I hadn't touched a gun in years. I held the .22 up to my face and took a closer look.

"Is this Dad's old peashooter?" I asked.

"Yeah."

"Good grief, it must be a hundred years old." I slipped my finger into the loop and flipped open the cylinder. No bullets. John slid a box of shells on top of the refrigerator.

"I thought Alice had this pistol," I said. Alice had borrowed it from Dad when she'd moved into an apartment in a bad neighborhood.

"She had it for a while. Then Stewart borrowed it to shoot at raccoons. I think Doris Ann had it after that."

I looked at John. "How did you get it?"

"I needed it to go fishing."

"To go fishing?"

"Yeah," he said. "I didn't want to throw one of my good pistols in that junked-up fishing-tackle box."

I looked down the barrel of the pistol. It was rusty and would probably have blown the hand off anyone foolish enough to shoot it.

"You shot the fish?"

"No, smart-ass," John said, thumping me on the head, "but you never know what's going to happen. Crazy people are everywhere."

Lewis didn't show up a single time during John's visit. But as soon as he left, the stalking began again. Lewis drove by my apartment several times a day, showed up at school under the pretense of looking up old friends, called all hours of the night. Even though I had a peace bond against him, he showed up at my graduation from Ringling School of Art & Design.

Throughout my last year at Ringling, I had been applying to graduate school. I'd been accepted at several universities and had been offered tuition scholarships by two of them. I chose the one that I thought would be the safest place to raise a teenager—and the one that was farthest away from Lewis. In the dead of night, I fled to the Midwest.

PART 3

Des Moines, Iowa

fate

I pulled the U-Haul into Mother's yard about noon the next day.
Alabama was halfway to Iowa, a good stopping point. But once
I felt the familiarity of being with family, I couldn't muster the
energy or courage to keep moving north. I slept for a week. Then
another. Mother eventually realized I wasn't going to make it to
graduate school without a push. One morning she said, "I've asked
Stewart to go with you to Iowa. Is that all right with you?"

Relief flooded through me. "Thanks, Mom. That would be great."

My big brother Stewart had started drinking in his midtwenties.
It became a problem in his thirties. Through the years, he was on and
off the bottle. Mother had told me several weeks ago that he was trying, once again, to quit. Weeks of sobriety had left him shaky and a
little anxious. He desperately needed something to occupy his time,
and I desperately needed his help.

Jason was thrilled that Stewart was coming along. He knew Stewart and I would talk. When Jason was younger, I'd send him outside
when I got together with my brothers and sisters because our conversations invariably gravitated toward our wild childhood and stories
of Dad's drinking. But Jason was thirteen now and needed to know
more about his grandparents, his aunts and uncles—and his mother.

As we drove out of Alabama, Stewart started talking, and talked
on, as if he'd needed the distance in order to see his life clearly.

"Every time I take a drink I feel like I'm doing something good for
myself," he said. "I know that sounds crazy. I know it's killing me. But

the moment I take a drink—God, it feels like I'm saved. All the pain inside my chest drains away."

"But you're not going to drink anymore, are you?" I blurted.

"No. Absolutely not. This time I'm done. I know I'm just like Dad, but I can beat it."

"You're not just like Dad."

"I inherited his alcoholic gene."

That was hard to argue. Still, unlike Dad, Stewart didn't take his anger and frustrations out on other people. To my knowledge, he'd never hit anyone in his life.

I said, "Do you remember the day I was at your house and Dad came in drunk?"

Stewart chuckled, and Jason, in the backseat, leaned forward so he could hear better.

"He didn't knock," I continued, "just barged in, leaving the door wide open. We were sitting around the woodstove drinking hot tea; you and me. You got up to put more wood on the fire. Dad staggered over, pointed at you, and said, 'I'll whip your ass.' You looked at him and said, 'All right. Give me a minute to load the stove, and we'll fall out into the yard.' By the time you shoved two pieces of wood into the stove, Dad had pulled up a chair and was warming his hands. He didn't mention fighting again."

Stewart nodded, and we both laughed.

"Yeah," Stewart said, "that was before I got to drinking so bad."

It was true that Stewart drank like Dad, much worse really, but I thought that maybe it was heartache he'd inherited more than alcoholism. I recognized the heartache because I had inherited it too; I didn't know how to soothe mine either.

Dad's life had been an ocean of loss. His mother died when he was a child, and he was shuffled from one older sibling to another, always unwelcome. At fifteen, he lied about his age and joined the military. As soon as he finished one tour, he'd reenlist, switching from the Merchant Marine to the Navy to the Marine Corps. But if he'd had a chance for survival, World War II took it away. I don't know everything that happened to him, but I know that he was shot and bayoneted and sent to a MASH unit. And I know the doctor there felt the only way to save his life was to amputate his infected right arm. But Dad found a weapon and stood him off. God knows what else happened to him over there. (He wouldn't say.) They sent him stateside, not expecting him to survive the trip. He returned home from the Pacific wounded and angry.

Dad had plenty to be angry about, but he displaced it on us. Mother made excuses for him, saying he suffered from nightmares and night sweats and drank to ease the pain.

Some of my earliest memories are of cringing under the covers in the dark because Dad was yelling at Mother. To comfort myself and to block out the noise, I rocked my head back and forth, back and forth. Not Stewart. He'd get out of bed and pace the floor.

When he was ten years old, he said, "I'm never going to drink." At twenty, he declared the same thing. He lost his way somewhere between twenty-five and thirty, and I could tell from the onset that it puzzled him.

As we drove out of Alabama, crossing into Tennessee, Stewart mused, "That alcoholic gene." He nodded toward Jason in the backseat. "Are you watching him?"

"Like a hawk," I answered.

We drove into Des Moines, Iowa, on a hot July night and stopped at a motel on the east side of town. We climbed out of the car, stretching and moaning with exhaustion, and Stewart immediately spotted something dripping from the back bumper of the car.

"What is it?" I asked.

He ran his hand along the bumper and held it out. Bright yellow oil slipped down his fingers.

He said, "I don't know what that is," just as I cried, "Oh, no." I popped the trunk on the car. My oil crayons had melted in the Iowa heat. Red oil rolled down the length of the bumper, and yellow dripped from the trunk. A puddle like a liquid moon formed on the hot black pavement. Jason stuck his finger in the pool and drew a line.

"I thought it was supposed to be cold up here," he said.

"It is," I said. "Apparently not in July." I thought about the wool sweaters that had been packed next to the art supplies and hoped they hadn't been stained with oil.

Jason wrote his initials in the yellow puddle. "I wanted to make a snow angel." He stood up and put his hands on his hips. The three of us looked around in unison. Even though it was close to midnight, we could see heat waves shimmering under the streetlights.

Stewart pointed out a cornfield that surrounded the motel. "Knee-high by the Fourth of July."

"What?" I asked.

"The corn. It's supposed to grow knee-high by the Fourth of July. I guess it made it." We walked over and stared at the tall green stalks. Alabama grew corn, but not like this. These thick broomstick stalks waved kitelike leaves of shamrock green. Even though there wasn't a bit of breeze, the corn rustled as if whispering secrets. Between the stalks danced the catchable light of fireflies.

That night, Stewart and Jason slept like stones, but I barely closed my eyes. The motel wasn't in a good neighborhood, and every noise sounded like a vandal on the prowl. I counted my money, made written projections on how long it would last, and murmured prayers, asking for guidance and a place to live. Early in the morning, I fell asleep and dreamed we were standing in the parking lot again, admiring the green summer corn, when it started to snow. The snow drifted silently down in dime-size flakes, settling on our heads and shoulders, and the snow-dusted cornstalks rustled, whispering our fate.

As soon as it was light enough, we drove over to see the Drake University campus, where I'd be spending my days as a graduate student. In the early-morning haze with a pale, fingernail moon overhead, it looked like something from a Gothic novel.

"Wow," Stewart said. "You can afford to go here?"

"No," I answered.

The next day, Stewart had to head for Alabama because he was due back at work. "I wish I could stay and help you find a place to live," he said. "I feel bad about leaving you here."

"I'll be fine," I said, but my entire body trembled with anxiety. It took every bit of willpower I possessed not to break down and go back home with him.

Stewart wrapped his arms around me, and I buried my face in his shoulder. He patted my back, then caught my shoulders and held me at arm's length as if to take a look at me. "Good luck, little sister."

I choked back tears. "I need more than luck. I need magic."

Stewart nodded. "Yeah, me too."

rescue

A few days after Stewart left for Alabama, Jason and I moved into a duplex apartment on the north side of Des Moines. It was a good neighborhood, and our duplex was the only rental property in the area. It was about a mile from Drake University, and Jason's school was within walking distance. The houses around us were built for raising children—two-story, fenced backyards—but the children must have all grown up and moved away. From the upstairs window in my bedroom, I could see forever. The land lay flat, and sparse. No rocking chairs cluttered the front porches, no vines climbed the railings. Neighbors didn't wander over unannounced. Even in the summer heat, no kids played in the sprinklers.

In the South, moving into a new home is a community event. Neighbors bring over sandwiches and blackberry pies, and stand around talking while you unload furniture. At one point, while we were moving into our Des Moines duplex, Jason asked, "Where is everybody?"

The next day, he announced, "This is like a ghost town."

Scared, broke, and horribly lonely, I longed for Stewart to come back, listened for his knock on the door. The ridicule I'd have to face for running back home suddenly didn't look so bad. I called Mother.

"Send Stewart to get me," I begged.

"Oh, honey, give it six months," she said. "Give it six months, and if you still hate it, then come home."

I started to cry. "But there's nothing here! It's flat. And the sun hurts my eyes. The sky goes all the way to the ground. There's no mountains. Everything's in a straight line. And it looks like somebody swept it."

"What are you talking about?"

"The ground!" I sobbed. "It's clean. It looks like somebody swept it. There's no junk. I don't know what they did with all the junk. And there's hardly any people. And no black people at all!"

"Honey, you're just homesick," Mother said. "It'll be all right. When do classes begin?"

"Two weeks," I cried. "Two weeks of nothing."

The next day Mother put my baby sister, Janet, on a plane to Iowa to help me get over the blues.

Unbeknownst to her, Janet had rescued me before—simply by being born. I was twelve years old, the middle child of seven; Janet was number eight. I was too common a sight for my parents to appreciate, for anyone to appreciate. But, oh! This new baby sister with her sharp smiling eyes! She thought I was gold! To show my appreciation, I drew pictures for her. Cats, bunnies, paper dolls. And family portraits: Dad, Mom, Alice, Stewart, David, me, Willie, Doris Ann, John, and Janet—all standing in a row, holding hands, like a crooked fence. In 1967, on the day she was born, I made a card for her, a drawing of Leonardo da Vinci's *The Last Supper*, which I traced from the large, gilded-framed rendition that Dad had bought for Mother.

I plugged in Dad's not-to-be-touched light-up picture of *The Last Supper*, stood on a kitchen chair, and spread six sheets of taped-together typing paper over the image. Even through the paper, it looked as if you could reach right through the glass and touch the figures. Jesus glowed and his halo radiated beams of fiery light. I studied his serene face, his outstretched arms, then taped the paper to the glass. The large, box-shaped picture tilted with my weight, and I steadied it on its nails and leaned back to admire the scene.

My brother David came into the living room and stood behind me. "Dad's going to kill you."

Blood rushed to my head. I shot him an ugly look, pulled a sharpened pencil from behind my ear, and began tracing Jesus' head.

"What are you doing?" he asked.

"I'm making a birthday card for Janet."

David laughed. "She just got born. She don't want no card."

I traced around Jesus' halo. "You don't know that. Besides, it's going to be really pretty when I'm done with it."

David laughed again. "Dad's going to kill you."

"Dad's at the hospital with Mother. And if you tell on me, I'll tell on you."

David scoffed. "Tell on me for what?"

"For smoking."

"I haven't been smoking," David shouted.

I shrugged. "Dad doesn't know that."

David kicked my chair and slammed out the front door.

I took a deep breath and began tracing: Peter, James, John, Andrew, and Judas, drawing faces first while the pencil was still sharp enough to capture their serious expressions. My arms ached, and staring at the bright image hurt my eyes.

Doris Ann wandered in. "Dad's going to kill you."

"He's at the hospital with Mother. And if you tell on me, I'll tell on you."

Doris Ann put her hands on her hips. "I haven't even done anything."

"I'll tell him you put that hole in the couch."

"Huh," she said. "Stewart put that hole in the couch."

I looked over my shoulder. "Dad doesn't know that."

"I'm gonna go tell Alice," Doris Ann said, and she stormed away.

Beads of sweat collected on my forehead. My fingertips made smudges on the paper. I drew the table and the disciples' sandaled feet underneath, their toes like little sausages.

John slammed through the front door. "Man, are you going to get it."

"If you tell on me, I'll tell Dad you were smoking."

"I'm only seven!" John cried.

"Scram."

My neck hurt. Sweat trickled down my back. The lightbulb inside the picture burned hot. The tape began to curl away from the glass.

Jesus glowed. Chalice, tablecloth, windows, walls. The hot glass burned my fingers. I traded hands and drew with my right, knowing the lines wouldn't be as crisp. Bread, wine. I peeled the drawing from the glass, jumped down, and quickly unplugged Dad's not-to-be-touched light-up picture of *The Last Supper.*

I spread the drawing on the floor, switched the pencil back to my left hand, and wrote, *To Janet Lynn, from her sister.*

Now Janet was on a plane to Iowa, supposedly to help me "set up housekeeping." Jason and I had been living out of cardboard boxes for years; it didn't take long to put the dishes away and stack our T-shirts on the floor. But I watched the clock, anticipating her arrival.

Jason and I picked her up at the airport. She threw her arms around us, and said, "Wow, from the sky, this place looks like a giant patchwork quilt!"

That evening, she praised my bravery, told Jason silly jokes, and insisted that we find something fun to do that would help us embrace this strange new land. The next day, we went to the art museum and, when we tired of that, bought tickets to the Iowa State Fair and went four days in a row. It was enormous! We'd been to fairs before, but nothing like this. Here there were rides, live music, animals, and exhibits, including a juried art exhibition. We saw the biggest pig in the world, a tractor pull, horse races, and the Strong Man competition. We rode the sky lift from one end of the grounds to the other and meandered our way back through exhibition barns, buying junk food along the way. Janet munched on popcorn and pointed out Iowa's good qualities.

"This is the best popcorn I've ever eaten," she said. "What do you think they did to it?"

I pointed to a cornfield in the distance and said, "I think they grew it right out there in that field."

Mother's plan worked. By the time Janet left, I agreed to give it six months, conceding that any state that annually commissions an artist to sculpt a life-size cow out of butter is one worth taking a chance on. But really my decision was made the moment my mother bought my sister's plane ticket. This was not a woman with the money for spontaneous cross-country trips. She'd never been on a vacation in her life. She worked, raised her children, and was at present helping raise her grandchildren. Yet she was so sure I could succeed in this dream of becoming an artist that she'd scraped up enough of her hard-earned money to invest in my transition to graduate school. It was clear she thought continuing my education was the way to save myself.

Janet flew back to Alabama, and the beginning of school brought the relief of structured days for Jason and me. Almost overnight, the temperature dropped from scorching to freezing. Jason cut his long blond hair and traded his flowered shorts for blue jeans. He started spending his free time playing basketball with his classmates. The advent of full-blown winter came much earlier than I expected. I learned to drive on snow-covered roads and finally understood the usefulness of a scarf. We adjusted. But somehow, I felt lonelier in Iowa than I had in Florida.

In an effort to fill the void left by my absent family, I stormed the local museums and art galleries. Des Moines had an active art scene and I was determined to be a part of it. At an opening for Iowa landscape painters, I met a woman wearing black leather pants, a black sweater, black boots, and bright purple gloves. Her hair matched her sweater and her eyes matched her gloves. I adored her immediately.

To introduce me into her circle of friends, Ann gave a luncheon and served quiche, which I'd never had before. I had almost nothing in common with these women. They came from privileged middle-class homes with normal parents, had suffered few childhood traumas, and knew little about alcoholism. But Ann and her friend Melanie were also artists, single, and struggling—and that was enough to feel understood. Quickly, Ann and Melanie became my friends, great girlfriends, of a sort I'd never had before, and I was delighted and honored to be part of their world.

neighbors

Despite our skeptical beginning, Jason and I eventually learned to love our home in Des Moines, Iowa. For the first time in years we felt safe. But our neighbors hated us. We were the only renters on the block, and Jason was the only child. Our neighbors were retired, and they spent their time tending their yards. Carefully manicured, velvet-green grass spread evenly from house to house and ended—square in the middle of the block—with us. My lawn mower didn't work, and I didn't have time to give my hedges a poodle cut. As soon as we moved in, the neighbors began to complain: *your son walks through my yard, please shovel the snow from your sidewalk, your grass needs cutting.* It was petty stuff, and nothing we did improved the situation. One morning as I headed for school, the man next door, a retired automobile salesman, shouted at me. He had been walking around his yard digging up crabgrass with a spade and scattering the spots with new grass seed. "Hey, you, when are you gonna kill the weeds in your yard?"

Annoyed, I opened my car door, tossed my books onto the passenger seat, and looked over the car roof to study my yard. "What weeds?"

He pointed with his spade. "Weeds. Right there. Millions of 'em, by God."

Four days earlier a kid had come by, pushing his lawn mower door to door, drumming up business. I paid him ten bucks to cut the grass. But since then, as if by magic, dandelions had sprouted everywhere. I couldn't afford to do anything about the little yellow blossoms that now made the lawn look like a piece of polka-dot cloth.

"Those aren't weeds," I said, climbing into the car. "Those are flowers." I drove away, headed to class, then work, furious that this man of leisure was adding to my stress. I thought about the blossoming dandelions and wished they covered his yard too.

When I was ten years old, we lived, for a while, in a house on Thirteenth Avenue in Birmingham. Our house was the only rental for several blocks, and our neighbors hated us then too. If they spoke to us at all, they said, "Too many kids. You're ruining the neighborhood." Our front porch was cluttered with rocking chairs, toys, and car parts; the front yard was worn down to the red clay by tennis shoes, bicycles, and dogs; and our backyard was a jungle of healthy weeds. The older couple who lived to the left of us, an insurance salesman and his wife, hadn't spoken to us at all in almost a year. I was surprised when the man suddenly asked me one day if he could pay me to pull all the weeds from the cracks in his sidewalk.

"Get your little brother and sister to help you," he said, winking at me, "and I'll pay you well."

Willie, Doris Ann, and I went to work. It was hot August, and the weeds were well established. Using Mother's table knives, we dug up every bit of green that grew between thirty or so flat squares of concrete. The backs of our necks and shoulders burned bright red. We expected to get paid at least a quarter apiece. We each got a nickel.

Willie stared at the five-cent piece in his palm. "That cheapskate," he complained. We pocketed our nickels and stared at each other. Then we giggled, and dashed into our backyard—a jungle of crabgrass, chickweed, beggar-ticks, and dandelions. We picked a handful of seeded dandelions each, then ran back to our neighbor's house and blew the fluff all over everywhere. We laughed, knowing that, come spring, he'd have a million immortal yellow blossoms sprouting from daggerlike leaves all over his perfectly manicured lawn.

As I drove to Drake University, I envisioned blowing the seeded dandelions all over my neighbor's yard. Like mushrooms, the spiky green weeds would pop up overnight.

By the time I got home from work that evening, the dandelions in my yard were dead. My neighbor had poisoned them. The air reeked of chemicals.

After that incident, that family wouldn't speak to us anymore. When they wanted to complain, they left a note on the door while I was at school. Our apartment was rented through a property management company, so they couldn't call the owner. Instead, the neighbors took things into their own hands. Without permission from me, they chopped my backyard picnic table into kindling because they thought it was "an eyesore." They painted white the old wooden rocking chair on my front porch—also, apparently, "an eyesore." And my bucket-size gargoyle planter simply disappeared. (I had traded another student two etchings for that handmade planter.) All in all, I was just thankful they were too law-abiding to burn down our house.

It hurt my feelings that our neighbors didn't like us, but I didn't have a lot of time to dwell on it. I was in graduate school during the day and working in the evenings. I was exhausted.

thespian

*J*ust when the brakes went out on my car, Jason came down with mononucleosis. I didn't have the money for the doctor or to fix the car. I went to see my girlfriend Melanie.

As soon as she opened the door, I asked, "Can I borrow a hundred dollars?"

"Of course, you can borrow a hundred dollars," she said, taking my elbow and escorting me to a cozy chair in the living room. "Will that get you through?"

I nodded, knowing that it wouldn't. Melanie wrote me a check and took me to my bank to deposit it. As I waited in line for a teller, I looked around at the security cameras and the armed guard, wondering how difficult it would be to actually rob the place. I felt that desperate.

Jason's tonsils looked like rotting lemons, and his fever soared. The doctor put him on antibiotics and bed rest. Once his fever had spiked, it dropped to one hundred degrees and stayed there. On our third office visit, Jason wasn't any better.

"Has he been resting?" the doctor asked.

I gave Jason an I-told-you-so look, and he said, "I'm on the basketball team," as if that explained why he hadn't been in bed.

"Basketball, my foot!" the doctor yelled. He glared at me.

Rather weakly I said, "I've tried to keep him in bed." Truly, it was impossible. Even when he was in bed, he didn't rest; he played video games or repeatedly bounced the basketball against the wall, driving me insane.

The doctor pointed his ink pen at me. "If you were covered by some kind of insurance, I'd slap him in the hospital right now!" He wrote out another prescription and handed it to me. "I want him in here every week until I say otherwise." He pointed the pen at Jason then and said, "And you *rest!*"

As we walked out of the clinic, I counted in my head what it would cost to see the doctor every week. Even one visit was more than I'd ever be able to pay.

I unlocked the car, and Jason sulked into the passenger seat. I knew it wasn't a good time to bring it up, but I didn't know what else to do.

"I'm thinking about going down to Social Services," I said. "Maybe getting on food stamps for a little while."

"No way, Mom!" Jason shouted. "All my friends will know! The guys on the basketball team work at the grocery store!"

I felt the same way. How could I face the cashier at the supermarket with a fistful of food stamps? What if *my* friends found out?

My parents had never received government assistance. Never. Even with a houseful of kids, little money, and one crisis after another, pride prevented them from even considering it. That pride was passed down to us kids and as adults kept us from applying, even when we desperately needed help. But my present choices were clear: drop out of school or apply for government assistance.

I paid my taxes, I reasoned. So I put on my best dress and heels, smoothed my curly hair and tied it back with a ribbon, put on makeup, and went down to the Department of Social Services. I opened the door and felt a shiver—the scowl my dad would make at the word *charity*. The door closed behind me and thirty or more women turned and looked at me. I immediately realized I'd made a mistake dressing up. Everyone had on shorts and T-shirts. I considered leaving and coming back another day, but I needed help as soon as possible. I bit my lip and asked the receptionist for the appropriate forms. My hands trembled as I filled them out.

My caseworker looked me up and down, glanced at my information sheet, and looked at me again. I could tell that she thought I was trying to pull a fast one on the government. "I need to check on a few things," she said, leaving me in the waiting room. It was too late to take off my hose and heels. I slipped off my earrings, pulled the ribbon out of my hair, and wiped my lipstick on the back of my hand. Three hours later I was still sitting there.

When she finally called me into her office, I walked like a field hand in those heels and used my thickest Southern accent.

"Ain't it a pretty day," I said. She smiled and relaxed.

I told her my situation, mispronouncing a word or two, as she studied my application and jotted notes in the margin.

"You and your child qualify for Title XIX health insurance," she said.

"I appreciate it," I said, trying to stay in character.

"And, according to my calculations, one hundred and eighteen dollars a month in food stamps."

I dropped my head and fought back tears. My misuse of the English language was a put-on, but the desperation was real.

For my next appointment with Social Services, I wore ratty clothes, dirty sneakers, tied my hair in a red, cotton handkerchief stamped with a cigarette logo, and spouted Southern right off the bat. I wanted to come across as extremely needy but with possibilities. A guttersnipe with potential. The guy who saw me (a different caseworker) glanced at me when I came in the door and never looked up again. He filled out the papers and sent me home.

do unto others

We were the only family in our neighborhood that had ever received food stamps—and the postman made certain everyone knew about it. On food stamp delivery day, the man next door would shout at me, "That comes out of *my* pocket!"

How could I explain to my neighbors that I was doing the best I could? I imagined sitting down with them and explaining that I planned to contribute to society as soon as I got out of school. I wanted desperately to be accepted, to be part of the community. My mind ran in circles, confused by who I'd been in the past, who I was now, and who I planned to be in the future; three distinctly different people. And the person in the middle—the present me—needed financial help.

As embarrassing as government assistance was for me, it was truly a blessing. Overnight, we had enough food. And we had medical care. Jason saw the doctor every week to check his blood levels for the mononucleosis virus, and months later, when he started getting better, the doctor removed his tonsils. I don't know how we would have survived without this program. It still scares me to think about it. As a mother, I'm supposed to protect my child; and when I did not have the resources to do that, our government provided assistance. With all the criticism Social Services has received through the years, it's hard to think of them as heroic. But every day they help mothers feed and protect their children.

One day I stood in our doorway waiting for the postman—waiting for the food stamps. I had left school early to be home for the delivery because Jason often made it home before I did, and I still hadn't told him about going to Social Services. I told him that I'd gotten our health insurance through Drake University, which wasn't true. To spend the food stamps, I'd disguise myself—wear my mother's old glasses and tuck my hair under a baseball cap—and drive to a faraway grocery store. I always got out of the store as quickly as possible and never looked at anyone, including the cashier, for fear I'd be recognized.

So far, I'd been able to intercept the food stamps each month and tuck them into my purse without Jason suspecting.

That day, I watched the postman deliver our neighbors' mail, and when he reached our house, I stepped out onto the porch. The postman had the manila envelope from Social Services—the food stamps—in his hand. I reached for the envelope and he pulled it back as if to keep it, then thrust it toward me and said, "Here is your mail—much to my great grief and sorrow." As he stepped off the porch, he muttered, "Scamming off of society." It took a second for me to grasp the full measure of what he'd said. Tears spilled down my cheeks as I watched him deliver mail to the next house. When he headed back, I met him at the sidewalk.

"What did you say?" I asked.

"What?"

"What did you just say to me?"

The postman took another bundle from his bag and kept walking. "I don't know what you're talking about."

I followed him. "You handed me my food stamps and said, 'Here is your mail, much to my great grief and sorrow.' And then you said that I was 'scamming off of society.' Do you think I'm deaf? Do you think I *like* being on food stamps?"

The postman turned into another house. When he came back to the sidewalk, I was still waiting. "'Much to my great grief and sorrow.' That's what you said." I shook the envelope in his face. "This is all the food we'll have for the next three weeks. Do you think we should starve? We don't deserve to eat?"

The postman walked away again and I followed, getting angrier.

"*Scamming off of society.* You think you can just blurt that out and run away?" He kept walking. I followed. "If you don't talk to me, I'm going to call your supervisor and talk to him!"

The postman turned and shouted, "My daughter was murdered two years ago!"

"What?" I said, completely taken aback.

He choked back tears. "My daughter was murdered."

I opened my mouth to speak but nothing came out. *What do you say to that?* I guess it accomplished what he wanted; it stopped me in my tracks. He walked to the next house and delivered the mail, then on to the next. He didn't look to see if I was following him. He knew that I wouldn't. How can you report someone whose daughter was murdered?

That evening someone left a handwritten note on my door that read, *Food stamps come out of the taxpayer's pocket! Why should I have to raise your child?* I was furious and horribly embarrassed at the same time. Once again I thought about dropping out of school and getting a job. I wouldn't be able to make ends meet in Iowa. I'd have to go south. For a moment I envisioned myself back in Alabama. I turned on the stove and torched the note so Jason would never see it. The anger burned away, but the embarrassment remained.

The next day there was another note: *Your trash can must be off the street before sundown.* How was I supposed to get the trash can off the street before sundown if I didn't get home until after dark? This time it was the anger that remained.

The next day I took my trash can to school with me. Down the fluted base, I painted bright yellow and blue stripes, and I painted the top bright red. With black enamel paint I wrote Bible scripture on the base of the trash can, Matthew 7:12, *Do Unto Others As You Would Have Them Do Unto You.* And on the top I painted Mark 12:31, *Thou Shalt Love Thy Neighbor As Thyself.* Someone in the sculpture department had discarded a platform with a flat base and three short, uneven sides. I painted the platform black and wired the trash can onto it. I hauled the piece back home and put it in my front yard a few inches from the sidewalk. It looked pretty good—and by this time I was more concerned with the overall look of the artwork than the message intended for my neighbors. Our snow shovel was already bright yellow. I painted red polka-dots all over it and attached it to the back of the platform so that it shot into the air like a tree. On the inside scoop of the shovel I painted the words from Matthew 7:1, *Judge Not That Ye Be Not Judged.*

I expected the trash can sculpture to be removed before I got home the next day, but it hadn't been touched. In fact, I never found another note on my door. The trash can sculpture sat in my front yard for over a year.

PART 4

Anniston, Alabama

XXV

Behold, the grave of a wicked man,
And near it, a stern spirit.

There came a drooping maid with violets,
But the spirit grasped her arm.
"No flowers for him," he said.
The maid wept:
"Ah, I loved him."
But the spirit, grim and frowning:
"No flowers for him."

Now, this is it—
If the spirit was just,
Why did the maid weep?

STEPHEN CRANE

if the spirit was just . . .

Dad had never been good with pain. At least not when it was his. When we were kids, he relied on Mother to take care of him, no matter the damage. She sobered him up and sewed him up. But they'd gotten a divorce long before I left for art school.

In Iowa, I was more than just physically separated from my family. Siblings got sick, had surgery, wrecked cars, suffered any number of life-threatening events—without my knowing the full details. And it wasn't that I didn't call home. Alabama felt like a phantom limb; it left me with a gnawing ache. I talked to someone every week, my mother practically every day. Still, I heard it through the family grapevine that Dad had been in the hospital.

"I didn't want to worry you," Mother said. "I didn't want you to drop out of school and move back home."

In three weeks, I was to start my second year of graduate school—two years to go before I'd get my master's degree. "Exactly how sick is he?" I asked.

Dad had been diagnosed with lung cancer. The spot on his lungs was small, the size of a half-dollar, and the doctor planned to treat it with chemotherapy. Afraid Dad would die before I saw him again, I borrowed money from my friend Ann and bought two tickets to Alabama.

Jason was fifteen now, but as a toddler he had waited for my dad to come home from work and rushed him the minute he stepped in the door. Dad would tousle his blond hair, then scoop him up and bury his weather-beaten face in Jason's pale baby skin. "There's my good buddy," he'd say. They made a striking pair. And right from the start, Jason could see through Dad's abrasive behavior. Dad could tell a great story, play a mean hand of poker, and make an automobile engine sing like a top. But it was the dreamy tone of voice he used with Jason that won my son's heart—and mine too. He didn't talk baby-talk or coo; it was something else entirely, like the charm of deep-pitched wind chimes. It had made me blush with pride. Privately, I hoped that he had spoken so enchantingly to me when I was a baby, but I could remember only one such time as a child.

I was nine years old, and we lived in Birmingham. Mother was sitting at the kitchen table and Dad was standing on the other side, talking to her. I walked up beside Dad just as he put his hands on his hips, and his elbow poked me right in the eye. It hurt badly and I complained. Dad was genuinely surprised that he'd caught me in the eye, but instead of apologizing, he mumbled that I should be more careful and stay out of the way. Angry and reckless, I said, "Let's see how you like it," and jumped up and socked him in the eye. Dad exploded into a rage. I ran around the table to Mother—with Dad on my heels. He clenched his teeth and pulled back his fist, ready to pound me into the floor.

"Nobody lays a hand on me!" he shouted. "Nobody! I'll kill ya! I'll kill ya!" And I was sure he was going to kill me. I grabbed the sleeve of Mother's dress and cowered, shrieking. Mother didn't move. She didn't look at Dad or me. She sat perfectly still. Dad's face turned red, then purple. Fist pulled tight as a bow, he held it there for what felt like an eternity. Then he released it in one long breath: dropped his fist, held his chest for a moment, and stared down at me with a horrified look on his face. He left without saying another word. As soon as he was gone, I ran away from home. Mother sent Stewart to track me down and bring me back. When he dragged me into the kitchen, I was still shaking.

"Don't worry, honey," Mother said. "Your father would never hit you when he wasn't drinking."

That evening Dad came home drunk. He sent one of my brothers to get me. To my surprise, Dad apologized to me then—and in that elusive, dreamy tone of voice: "You'll forgive me, won't you, Southpaw? I wouldn't hurt you for anything, and I wouldn't let anyone else hurt you. I'm your daddy. I brought you into this world."

Of course, I told him he was forgiven, and I told him I was sorry too. Yet, it didn't make sense. He was awful all the time and he never apologized. Why was he apologizing now? It took a while to figure it out. Earlier in the day, when the incident had happened, Dad had been completely sober. As a sober man, he saw himself as my provider, my protector, my daddy. It was my first glimpse at how he saw himself, or at least how he wanted to be.

After that, when he drank and roared with anger, I tried to keep in mind the man with the enchanted voice, knowing that he was in there somewhere.

When I got to Alabama, I went to see Dad right away. I intended to visit him by myself, but several of my brothers and sisters invited themselves along. John was home from Germany on furlough from the Army, and he wanted to go. Janet hadn't spent much time with Dad since he and Mother had divorced—she said she didn't know how to talk to him—so she came along as well, knowing I could do the talking for both of us. And at the last minute, Stewart climbed into the car. He'd been drinking. He'd suffered through detox twice since he'd helped Jason and me move to Iowa, but he hadn't been able to stick to it. On that morning he was drunk out of his mind and drank more on the drive to Dad's house.

After Dad and Mother divorced, Dad remarried and moved into his new wife's home. When we got there, her miniature poodle met us at the door, barking like crazy.

"That's not a dog!" Stewart shouted. He leaned over it and barked back, a fit of high-pitched yapping that made us all cringe.

"Stop it, Stewart," I begged, and pulled on his arm. Stewart worked repairing military weaponry at the Anniston Army Depot; his arms felt like steel rods. When he pulled back, we almost toppled to the floor. He jerked away from me and shook his head vigorously at the dog so his shoulder-length, corkscrew curls fluffed out like a rag mop. The poodle barked hysterically. Dad's new wife kicked her fuzzy bedroom-slippered feet at Stewart and screamed in a high-pitched voice that matched the dog's, "Make him stop, S.K.! Make him stop!" Dad got out of his chair and walked to the end of his oxygen line and stopped short. As bad as I felt for him, I had to smile secretly at the pained look on his face. Oh, he was in physical pain all right, but at the moment, it was being hooked up to an oxygen machine, witnessing the ruckus between the dog, his oldest son, and his wife that was killing him.

Finally John took command: "Come on, Stewart. Let's go take a look at David's motorcycle." Stewart straightened up, pushed the curls out of his face, and looked around the room for our brother David. "He's not here," John explained. "The bike's in the garage. Dad's storing it for him."

As soon as they left, the dog calmed down and the room grew quiet. Everybody sat down at once. I sat across the room with Janet. On the drive over, she'd said, "I'm not mad at him. I just feel passed over. He never yelled at me like he did everybody else; he never threatened me; I didn't get anything at all. Sometimes I wish I'd been born the year after John, instead of almost eight years later." I'd said, "So he would have yelled at you too?" Janet had laughed and said, "Yeah."

I reached over and pinched her now, trying to get her to talk.

"Ouch," she said, rubbing her arm and giving me the bad eye.

I sighed, annoyed, and struck up a conversation about Jason. "Dad, Jason's playing varsity basketball this year."

Dad brightened. "He is?" He smiled and looked at the floor. "He's sure got the height for it. He *looks* like a basketball player."

"He's really good," I said. "I go to all of his games."

Stewart's voice echoed from outdoors, and we all looked in the direction of the garage. Janet got up to investigate and came back with a look of panic on her face. "Stewart wants to take David's motorcycle for a test drive."

"Oh, for Pete's sake," I said, grabbing my car keys. "He can barely walk. I'd better take him home before he gets himself killed."

"We'd better go save him from himself," Dad said, slipping the oxygen hose from around his neck and climbing from the couch. He put his arm around Janet and hugged her tight.

"Sorry, Dad," I said. "I was hoping for a longer visit."

He nodded and hugged me. As he walked us to the door, he winked at me, his green eyes sharp as nails. "I've got a portable oxygen tank. In the morning, I'll take you and Jason down the road for some bacon and eggs."

The phone rang at 6 A.M., and I expected it to be Dad, ready to go to breakfast. But it was my sister-in-law, David's wife.

"Barbara," she said, "your dad shot himself this morning."

I began to shake and an uncontrollable howl welled up from my chest. Mom ran into the living room to see what was the matter. My sister-in-law shouted into the receiver, "Barbara, he's not dead! Listen to me, he shot himself in the head but he's *not* dead. I need for you to round everybody up and get them over to the hospital. David has already gone down there. Call everybody else."

Everybody else meant the rest of my siblings: Alice, Stewart, Willie, Doris Ann, John, and Janet. I believe my sister-in-law told me Dad wasn't dead to buffer the shock. It worked. As I dialed the phone, I had an image of Dad with a bandage around his forehead—like a wounded GI right out of an old World War II movie, the bullet having only grazed his temple. Still, I struggled to dial the phone. When I told Janet, she screamed and threw the phone across the room. She was still screaming when I handed the receiver to Mother because I couldn't bear to listen to her pain. After that call, I couldn't say the words. I lied. I told Stewart and Willie that Dad had gotten sick during the night, that he was in critical condition.

As much as I tried to imagine that Dad was all right, the realization of what had happened slowly settled in, and I knew he was dead. Dad knew guns. He wasn't playing around. He intended to kill himself.

Mother hadn't reached that conclusion yet. She dressed and ran a comb through her hair. As soon as Willie and Janet arrived, she wanted to go to the hospital.

"The others can get there on their own," she said. "Let's go."

On the way to the car, she grabbed an orange daylily that was growing by the porch.

"Let's go," she said again, urging us into the car. Just then the phone rang. Mother ran back inside and answered it. We followed on her heels. A moment later she dropped the receiver into the cradle and said, "We've lost him. He's gone." She looked out the window and stared hard into the woods. Tears welled in her eyes but didn't spill down her face. We all started to cry at once. Even as distraught as I was, I could tell that Mother was somewhere else, lost in her thoughts. She dropped the flower beside the phone and spoke as if she was speaking only to herself, "That son of a bitch."

It was hard to believe that Dad was dead. After all those years of worrying that he'd crash while driving drunk, or that his liver would give out, or his heart. I would never have believed him capable of suicide. Nor would I have believed that a bullet could go straight through his temple and leave his head completely intact.

I sat through his funeral shaking so badly that when I spoke, my sentences didn't make sense. I was a grown woman. I thought I was safe from the bumps and bruises, confusion and suffering, caused by his drinking. When he pulled that trigger, I'm sure he thought he was simply ending his own struggle with pain, but that bullet traveled straight through each of his eight children as surely as if we'd been standing in a line beside him when the gun went off.

Jason didn't quite know how to react to Dad's death. At the graveside service, he banded with Janet and his cousins. I heard him whisper, "I don't understand why he would shoot himself."

Janet whispered, "Let's not talk about it anymore. It makes me shake."

In a hushed voice Jason said, "He was supposed to take Mom and me to breakfast that morning. Why would he make plans with us if he was going to kill himself?"

After the funeral, I sat in Mother's rocking chair and rocked frantically. It was the only way I knew to soothe the shakes. I was scared and angry, and by that time, feeling guilty. *If I had been paying closer attention, would he still be alive? If I hadn't ran off to art school? If I'd stayed home and watched after him?*

That night I resurrected a childhood comfort—rocking my head back and forth until I fell asleep. With a start, I woke up an hour later, drenched and shaking uncontrollably. I sneaked through the dark house, past Jason sleeping on the couch, and made my way into Mother's room. She had her back to me, and I thought she was asleep, so I slipped into her bed, something I'd never done before. She raised up and looked over her shoulder and asked, "Are you all right?"

Even though it was a warm summer night, I pulled the covers around my face. "I can't stop shaking."

Mother nodded and lay back. She was quiet, and I thought she was falling asleep. Then she said, "I'd like to kill him myself for doing this to my children."

I was astonished that Mother would say such a thing. Yet she had always been the one who held us tight, protected us. Dad had been charismatic, almost bigger than life, but his drinking made him dangerously unpredictable, and now, with his final act of violence, he had hurt us yet again.

free-falling

*T*wo days after Dad's funeral, Jason and I flew back to Iowa. I looked down from the airplane and felt as if I were free-falling. In Alabama, there are strip pits—land where miners excavate rock and sand and then abandon the hole in the ground. Eventually it fills with rainwater. My older sister, Alice, used to take us kids out to the pits to swim. In some places, the rock cliffs dropped thirty-five to forty feet down to the water. And the water was blue as blue. Reported to be bottomless. Stewart, David, Willie, Doris Ann, John, and I used to hold hands and run right off the bank. We'd scream all the way down even though we knew the water would catch us. We'd done it a thousand times. After Dad's funeral, on that plane ride back to Iowa, I had that same sensation. Free-falling—but without a safe landing in sight. I felt completely unprepared to leave Alabama and return to school in the Midwest. My mom, my brothers and sisters, they were the only people in the world whose faces reflected the same shock and loss as mine.

Classes began at Drake University two days after I arrived back in Iowa. Just to give my trembling hands something to do, I'd already started working on an etching: a robin sitting on a black hat. In my mind, Mother was the robin, Dad was the black hat. Together they hovered over a soybean field as if the hat were a magic carpet and the bird unable to fly on its own. I'd taken the trees from my early sketchbooks, the trees from my parents' backyard, and used them as a horizon line to give the image depth. The bird and hat, field and trees, brooded under a dark, starry sky.

I was standing by the press, mixing black ink on a slab with a palette knife, when my professor came into the printmaking studio. During the summers, he planted high-yielding vegetable gardens. In the fall, he brought in boxes of tomatoes, zucchini, and corn for his students. He was unaware that the students joked about this and shirked the vegetables. He was unaware that I—gladly—took home almost all of them.

He eased a huge box of tomatoes and cucumbers onto a worktable and walked over. "Already at work?" he asked, putting his hands on the other side of the counter and leaning in, studying the bird etched into the zinc plate. "This is new imagery."

I nodded.

He looked up. "How was your summer?"

I started to shake, but continued to stir the ink. I made eye contact for just a second, then looked away. "My dad committed suicide. Five days ago."

My professor paled, turned around, walked straight to his office, and shut the door. I slipped to the floor and cried until students began to fill the print studio. It seemed pointless to keep doing what I was doing. I had been trying to dig out of my ramshackle past with a teaspoon, and Dad's death had heaped on a fresh load of rubble.

falling

Stewart had taken a bottle of Jack Daniel's to Dad's funeral. Who could say anything to him? Not me. Secretly I was jealous that he had a way to deaden the pain. After that day, he doubled his intake, then tripled it. He drank in the morning, at noon, and at night.

Stewart climbed inside the military tank, waited for his eyes to adjust to the darkness, and studied the damage that needed to be mended. The fracture to the tank was long and deep. It would take hours to repair. He took in a long breath and studied an old welding seam, a fracture that had been repaired years earlier. It was smooth, strong. He reached out and touched the seam, recognizing the handiwork of his father, who had had this job before him. He took one more deep breath to steady himself and set to work.

Stewart flipped his safety helmet over his face, picked up a welding torch, and struck an arc. Starting at the top, he began to run a bead, flawless as ribbon, down the break. He was well-known for that skill. Satin welding. As he worked, tiny sparks burned holes in his T-shirt. He stopped, adjusted another rod into the welder, went back to work. The hot Alabama sun and the torch quickly heated the inside of the tank. Sweat ran down his neck and arms. Every time he picked up a new welding rod, he felt light-headed.

Stewart worked inside the tank all afternoon, intent on the job at hand, unaware of the climbing temperature. When the break inside the tank looked like a silver Christmas ribbon from top to bottom, he dropped his torch and helmet and climbed through the hatch into the open air. The sunlight pierced his eyes and the small white clouds overhead began to swirl. For a brief moment, stars sparkled in a black sky and then he fell, headfirst. His skull and jaw fractured when he hit the tank track, his nose and cheekbone when he landed facedown on the concrete floor.

Mother sat in the hospital emergency room with several other family members, waiting. When the doctor finally came out, she stood up. The doctor said, "He's got a concussion." He paused. "And we need to rebuild his face. But it's too dangerous right now. He's still drunk. He'll have to dry out first."

Drying out meant d.t.'s. Delirium tremens: tremors and hallucinations caused by alcohol withdrawal. The tremors came on hard and Stewart had to be restrained. Raging against the restraints, he burst the blood vessels in his eyes. Thirty-six hours without alcohol and he began to hallucinate.

"Bees!" Stewart screamed, pulling on the restraints. "Help me! They're killing me!" Spit collected in the corner of his mouth. "Mom! Mom! Help me!"

Mother told me Stewart had broken his nose. Not knowing the situation, I had laughed. "What did he do, walk into the wall?"

A few days later my younger sister Doris Ann called. Fear gripping every word, she said, "It was horrible. I thought he was going to die. He's in detox now, but he looks terrible; his face is all swollen and he's shaking like a leaf. And even though he knows it'll kill him, I think he'll drink as soon as he gets out."

"He's in the hospital?" I asked.

"Barbara!" Doris Ann shouted. "He almost died! His skull was fractured and his face was smashed!"

A shiver ran through me. "Mother said he broke his nose."

In tears, Doris Ann cried, "He completely lost his mind with the d.t.'s. He didn't even know who I was! He tried to break free; he said he was going to kill me!" Doris Ann blew her nose. "I'm not sup-posed to tell you any of this."

I felt sick, remembering that I'd laughed when I talked to Mother. Then a wave of anger ran through me. "Why didn't Mother tell me what was really going on?"

Doris Ann shouted, "'Cause she's afraid you'll quit school!"

I sucked in a sharp breath to keep from crying, feeling trapped.

Doris Ann's voice softened. "He's out of danger now. For the time being. Just stay there. I'll tell you everything. I'll tell you if you need to come home. You can't do anything anyway. None of us can."

I held the phone pressed against my ear as if it were a lifeline. Since Dad's death, something inside me had been off-kilter, as if the threads that held me together had suddenly begun to unravel. I could sense that same thing happening to Stewart—his lifeline fraying like a cut rope.

there was one I met upon the road

Alabama cicadas screamed the night Dad died. Weeks went by, and all the way back in Iowa, I could still hear the drone, a buzzing in my head. I went to school, to work, and home again, but only half-aware. I was still listening to the screaming cicadas.

Inadvertently, a graduate colleague provided me with a diversion.

"Barbara, you've got to meet this artist I've been telling you about," she said. "He's thirty-two, two years younger than you. He's got green eyes and black hair; he's *extremely* talented and crazy as *hell*. Schizophrenic. Been locked up so many times the nurses on the psych ward know his antics by heart." She laughed. "I met him at *church*. He renounced Catholicism to be a Mormon." She rolled her eyes. "Truly, he's one of the finest artists that I know. I told him I was staying with you for a few days before I headed home. I told him to come see us."

By the time Patrick stopped by, my friend had gone on to Utah. He stood in my doorway, every bit as handsome as she had said, and talked about making art. Normally, I would have been on guard. In fact when my graduate colleague had mentioned the famous Patrick before my dad died, I was completely uninterested in meeting him. His problems seemed too big to tackle. But Dad's suicide paralyzed my ability to think. I stood in the doorway, enchanted, listening to Patrick's words tumble musically from his perfectly shaped mouth.

Having been warned of his schizophrenia, I listened for signs of split personality, the only symptom of the disease that I was aware of, but I heard only the odd poetics of his speech: "If the spawning ground for young artists is a stony brook, one must hope there are enough still, deep pools along the way." He smiled, and I smiled back. We stood in the doorway for half an hour before either of us thought to sit down.

"Would you like to get some french fries?" he asked, pulling the rubber band from his long hair and letting it cascade onto his shoulders. No one had ever asked me if I wanted to "get some french fries" before. It seemed oddly specific. We drove to the local burger joint, sat on the picnic table out front, and ate fries from red-checkered boxes.

When I got back, Jason was waiting for me. He was standing in the driveway tossing a basketball into the hoop at the end of the parking area. When I got out of the car, he dropped the ball and walked over to meet me. He waved as Patrick drove away.

"So, is he crazy?" Jason asked.

"I don't know. He seems just fine. He wants to come over and take a look at that series of drawings I did on alcoholism."

"Oh, Mom," Jason complained, "you're not gonna date this guy, are you? Wasn't Lewis enough to steer you away from *crazies*?"

"No, no," I protested. "I'm not going to date this guy. And for your information, Lewis wasn't crazy. He was just mean."

"Yeah," Jason said, snatching up the basketball again, "mean enough to pick fistfights with our friends and smash the windows out of our house and follow you around for a year. Don't you remember that time he threw raw eggs at the drawings you had taped on the living room wall? He ruined a whole semester of drawings. We had to move all the way to Iowa just to get away from him. What's your definition of *crazy*?"

I blushed and stared at the ground.

Jason tossed the ball into the hoop. "So when's this crazy guy coming back to look at your art?"

"Next weekend, supposedly. But I wouldn't count on it."

The basketball bounced forward. Jason slapped it and tossed it into the air again. "Isn't schizophrenia split personality?"

"Yeah. Something like that."

"Well, when he says, 'I'm thirsty, and so am I,' you might want to run for your life."

defiance

*D*ad's death was a rock in my heart. As a sort of visual requiem for him, I went back to work on my drawings about alcoholism. In fact, the drawings had begun forming in my head within days after his funeral. When I started working, it felt as if I were attacking the paper with the pencil, and sometimes the paper began to unravel as I worked. I had ten finished drawings and decided to create ten more, using large, heavy sheets of paper that would hold up under duress.

For whatever reason, the images that came to me were inspired by an incident that happened one afternoon in April 1968. I was about fourteen, and had become my dad's driver. Dad didn't have a legal driver's license because of countless offenses for driving while intoxicated and attempting to outrun the law. He owned a 1960 antique-gold Cadillac with power windows and leather seats, and more likely than not, if he was riding, someone too young to have a driver's license was driving. When my older brothers, Stewart and David, joined the Marine Corps, I was next in line as chauffeur. As soon as I was tall enough to reach the pedals, he had me drive him to the bars. We roamed the back roads, seeking out watering holes in one-dog towns all over Alabama. On this particular April afternoon, the South was deep in the throes of the civil rights movement.

We were sitting in the driveway of the bootlegger Tombstone Crawford, waiting for a bottle of whiskey to be passed through the window. Tombstone was an eighty-year-old black man. It was rumored he'd been married several times, had a dozen kids, and had been a preacher, a cardsharp, and a gravestone carver. I had heard his name spoken with quiet reverence.

Since I'd become the driver, I'd been to Tombstone's place twice. He was an ancient little man with a face incised like a plowed field. When we'd visit, he'd pass a brown paper bag through Dad's window that contained a bottle of whiskey and occasionally tomatoes and okra from his garden. Sometimes he'd walk around to the driver's side and slip me a bag of salted peanuts. The last time we came by, I got brave enough to look into his eyes. They gleamed like polished stones, and his left eye had a pale blue oval shape right in the middle. It looked like a planet or a star. This time, I was hoping to get a better look at it. We drove into the driveway and I sounded the password—three sharp bleats of the horn—but nobody came out of the tar-paper shack.

Dad rolled down his window and dropped his arm down the side of the car. He drummed his fingers on the door. "Something's not right," he whispered.

"I can see kids looking out the window," I said, waving to them.

"Something's not right. Let's get out of here. Back up, Barbara. Let's go." He cocked his head to check behind us.

Knowing that Dad had a sense for trouble, I put the car in reverse and began to back out of the driveway. I had only moved a couple of feet when Tombstone came out of the house. He walked across the yard, holding a large grocery sack, cinched at the top.

Dad pulled his billfold from his back pocket. "Howdy," he said, but Tombstone didn't take his eyes from the sack. He slid it through the open window onto Dad's lap and turned back toward the house.

"Hey," Dad shouted, and rapped against the car with the money in his fist. "Hey!" He looked over at me. "What the hell . . ." He watched Tombstone go back inside, then looked behind us again. "Let's get out of here," he said, tossing a ten-dollar bill into the air. It tumbled in the red dirt and settled against a broken concrete block by the steps.

I backed out of the driveway onto the blacktop and headed down the road. We drove in silence for a minute. Dad pushed the button to raise the window. He cleared his throat and shook his head. "What the hell's gotten into him?" He mused for a moment longer, then said, "Humph," and began to uncinch the paper sack. "Jesus Christ!" he shouted, jerking his hands away from the sack. "Stop the car, Barbara. Stop the car!"

I slammed on the brakes. "What is it?!"

"There's something in this bag," Dad shouted. "Something alive!" He threw open the door before the car had stopped and jumped out. The paper sack fell from his lap onto the road. The whiskey bottle cracked as it hit the pavement, soaking the bag. Whiskey rivered onto the ground. I backed up, put the car into park, and leaned across the passenger's seat to take a look. Dad jumped onto the door frame and held on to the open door. The bag on the road beneath him was alive with the musical sound of castanets and a bulging, sagging rhythm. The soggy paper gave way, and out crawled an angry, whiskey-soaked snake. A rattlesnake.

"Jesus Christ!" Dad shouted, climbing into the car and slamming the door. "Jesus Christ."

The front page of the *Birmingham News* that day carried this headline:

> *Reverend Dr. Martin Luther King Jr. Is Slain in Memphis;*
> *A White Suspected; Johnson Urges Calm*

Shortly after Dad died, that event came rushing back to me. The obvious questions came to mind: *What if the snake had bitten Dad? What if he had died? How would our lives have been different?* As I thought about that day, other questions occurred to me: *Did Tombstone intend to kill Dad? Did he consider it retribution for what happened to Dr. King? And why a snake?*

Of course, there were no answers to my questions. Still, when I thought about Tombstone and that whiskey-soaked snake, it made me smile. Something about his behavior felt familiar, like something I might have done had I been in his situation. Tombstone wormed his way into my heart that day, and the angry rattlesnake slithered into my artwork. Huge diamondbacks curled onto the paper and spit venom. I scribbled with dark charcoal pencils around and around the snake until the background was a mass of tangled lines that almost completely swallowed the images. Sometimes that rattlesnake represented my dad, other times it represented justice. But as the drawings developed, that rattlesnake began to symbolize my own desire to fight back. I used it as a means to silently shout, *Don't tread on me.*

walking in the sky

*P*atrick skidded into my yard, unannounced, on a beat-up motor-cycle. He was haggard and disoriented and needed a place to stay for the night. He untied a bundle from the back of the motor-cycle, came inside, ate dinner, took a shower, and sat on the couch all evening without saying a word. I didn't mind. I felt the same way myself. Shell-shocked. I climbed the stairs to bed, leaving him on the couch, staring into the darkness.

I went into Jason's room to check on him before I went to bed. He was playing a video basketball game and didn't take his eyes from the TV screen when I bent down to kiss him on the forehead.

"He's a nut, Mom."

"Well, that makes two of us."

One night turned into several. Patrick was in such bad shape that I couldn't bring myself to ask him to leave. Then one day he left as suddenly as he had appeared, and I wasn't sure I'd ever see him again. Days later he came back—and he couldn't remember where he'd been. His clothes were rumpled, as if he had been sleeping in them; he needed a shave, and he was thinner than when we'd first met.

Patrick scared me a little bit, but I was still glad to see him. This time he brought a journal and a sketchbook filled with crayon draw-ings: colorful abstracts, young girls with erotic lips, furniture designs. I was taken aback by the beauty of his work: patches of color outlined in black charcoal that flicked around the subject like fireflies. I was truly enamored with Patrick's talent. But of all the things that drew me to him, none was more attractive than his need for care. He was like a baby bird that had fallen from its nest.

That night, while I cooked dinner, Patrick used my art supplies. He taped a full sheet of rag paper onto my drawing board and set to work. I watched him for a minute before I retreated to the kitchen. He was so at ease, so flip about the process. It always took me five minutes just to get up enough nerve to make a mark on a new sheet of paper. Later, Patrick brought the drawing board into the kitchen and sat it against the wall. I couldn't believe how quickly he had worked. And it was lovely. *Making Love Backwards* was written across the bottom of the drawing. I ran my fingers along the edge of the paper and burst into tears.

After dinner, we sat on the front porch. Patrick stared into space for an hour, then suddenly talked on and on. . . .

"Although my basic premises and convictions have not changed for many years, the manner and type of negotiating I utilize to manage such is changing. The calamity of my view is that the solution exists at arm's length to anyone. Our forefathers have more than provided ample opportunity for any individual to cultivate an appreciative amount of common sense. But for the sake of pride and greed and just plain indulgence do these opportunities go unattended. I've somewhat allowed the outside world to see its own lubricious activities in myself, experiencing such a level of repulsion to it myself at times; mocking such with antics is a simple expression of anger and resentment. From there it can get about as involved as a person desires. A well-sought-out common sense and goodwill in myself is so terribly tormented and frustrated in a basically childish and dangerously excessive world."

The next morning I went through his belongings and found a bottle of Navane. Patrick had told me that he carried the medicine, an antipsychotic drug, with him, but that he didn't take it. He said he didn't need it, there was nothing wrong with him. I couldn't help but wonder why he carried medicine with him if he really believed he didn't need it. And it was obvious that he did.

Starting the next day, I put 5 mg of Navane in his grits every morning. He loved grits. He thought the whole Southern thing beguiling and romantic. And if the Navane changed the taste of the grits, well, being a Yankee, he didn't know what they were supposed to taste like anyway.

When the Navane took effect, he improved rapidly. We planted a garden and did yoga exercises together, flirting as we held a pose. We talked about art and the world in sentences that made sense and drew large charcoal drawings of each other. Patrick's drawings made me look beautiful. Not model beautiful. Everything beautiful. The lines he used flowed like water, like a river. I stared at the drawings, delighted that he had created such beauty from the likes of me.

Jason had given up pointing out the obvious problems with this relationship. He had come to like Patrick—and I had stopped crying about my dad's suicide. So Jason pitched in and went along with whatever notion I had for survival: his, mine, and Patrick's.

During those first few weeks that Patrick stayed with us, Jason and I would come home from school to find Patrick waiting to show us new drawings. Occasionally he sent small ones to me like postcards. He walked them down to the local postal box so I would receive them, unexpectedly, in the mail. Checking the mail became an excitement. Rather than mindlessly shuffling through and tossing the bills into a box, I flipped through in search of his brightly painted hieroglyphics, indecipherable messages, and burning love poems.

He'd surprise me with other gifts—huge bouquets of wildflowers; meticulously carved jack-o'-lanterns; old, musty books of fairy tales. Sometimes he'd read the old books out loud and act out the parts. It was better to spend my evenings in Patrick's fantasy world than to cry all night over my dad's suicide, wasn't it?

Every night we made a production of dinner. I got out a box of never-used china, one of the few items I had managed to keep from my last failed marriage. Each plate had a circle of small, pale flowers in the center and was edged with fourteen-karat gold. We cooked pasta and picked baby greens from our garden for the salad. We sipped hot tea and made plans. Jason talked about basketball games and girls. I talked about my job in the art office at the university. I hoped the Art Department chair would give me a good recommendation when I looked for a job after graduation. Patrick mentioned getting a job and renting a studio. He had seen my studio space at the university and wanted something similar, a place to work other than on my kitchen table.

The Navane hit its mark, and Patrick got a job with Roth Goodwin Design, a firm where he had worked several times before. When I met Mike Roth, the owner of the firm, he said, "Patrick's worth the risk. He's liable to disappear at any time; in fact we worry whenever he leaves for lunch. But when he's working, when he's on, he's as good as it gets."

For me, at least for a while, we felt like an accidental family. I fell into Patrick like a stone into a well. My focus shifted from my life to his. And even though I knew Patrick had serious problems, I desperately needed that sense of family.

I was raised to believe that public displays of affection were unseemly. I can count the times that I saw my father kiss my mother's cheek—and I never saw my mother kiss him in front of us kids. In fact, when I was a teenager, I believed that she didn't love him. Then one Sunday morning—I was nineteen and had just moved back into their house after my first marriage ended—I opened their bedroom door and saw my mother snuggled against my father's back with her arms wrapped around his chest. She was kissing his neck. They startled when they saw me and jumped apart, but I had seen the looks on their faces. They weren't thinking about their children and grandchildren asleep in the next rooms, or the bills. They had transcended all of that. Of course, I immediately shut the door, but I never forgot the glimpse of what they privately shared.

Even though I had been married twice by the time I met Patrick, I hadn't fully understood the intimacy I'd witnessed that day until I fell in love with him. And once it was there, I understood my mother's inability to let it go. Having grown up in the sixties and seventies, I'd heard about addictive drugs like heroin and cocaine. I imagined that it was the same sensation, that feeling of letting go—like a single drop of rain finding the ocean.

guiding me backward

After Patrick had been at my house for a while, I thought we might become lovers. I thought, sometimes, that he was as attracted to me as I was to him. The Navane seemed to be working, he had gotten a job, and he was so handsome and talented. Up to that point, we had only flirted with a physical relationship. But one Friday evening Jason went to stay the night with a friend. Patrick and I were on our own. I was excited. I hadn't been involved with anyone since moving to Iowa. I poured raspberry juice into wineglasses, ran a bath, undressed, and invited Patrick into the tub with me. He was lying on my bed with his arms under his head, fully clothed, and I stood in the doorway, nude. He never looked at me. He said, "I don't have to do a damn thing I don't want to do." I had seen Patrick turn cold before, but nothing had prepared me for this. I stood for a moment, stunned, then pulled on a sweatshirt and jeans. Patrick sat up on the bed as I dressed.

"Who do you think you are?" he sneered. "Nobody tells me what to do. I'll do as I damn well please." I shoved on my tennis shoes. Patrick yelled, "Look at you! Who would want to take a bath with you anyway?!"

"I'm going to my studio!" I shouted. "And I don't want you here when I get back!" I ran down the stairs, grabbed my car keys, ran out the door, and climbed into my car. I cried, shaking with hurt and anger, and struggled to get the key in the ignition. I finally started the car and began pulling out of the driveway, but before I got to the street,

Patrick opened the passenger side door and climbed in. He wrapped his arms around me and said, "Don't go." I burst into convulsive sobs. Patrick rocked me gently, and then angrily he said, "Look what they've done to you. Just *look* what they've done to you."

What they? I thought. But somehow he convinced me to come back inside with him.

After talking for hours, we finally took that bath. I eased my back against him and he wrapped his arms around me, pressing them over my breasts. And when we stepped from the tub, he pushed his wet body against mine, and eased us, still dripping, into the bedroom. The bathwater had been cool, but steam rose from his chest and neck. Goose bumps climbed my arms and then subsided as his heat became mine. He crushed my lips with his, then slid his tongue down my neck and bit the curve of my shoulder, guiding me backward onto the bed. He whispered, "You're beautiful, you know?"

But I didn't know. Suddenly I was aware of my thin body, my less than perfect face, and I had to will myself not to reach for a blanket to hide under. He sensed my discomfort and pushed the pillows and blankets from the bed. "You *are* beautiful," he said as he lightly ran his fingers from my chin to my thigh. He eased his body onto mine, his weight soothing like a drug, dispelling waves of fear and loss and loneliness. Our fingers interlocked and our arms stretched out until we lay in the shape of a cross. He kissed my mouth, and I kissed him back, pliantly, as good judgment slipped away—exchanged for passion, exchanged for the intensity that pooled like blood in his irises.

I closed my eyes and surrendered to the unknown, gave myself over to him as completely as I had, as a child, given myself to Jesus, and with that same hope—hope for washed-clean healing that transcended even passion. By morning he was necessary, something I had to have in order to live.

angel

I didn't drink alcohol then, not even beer. If nothing else, my father had been a perfect example of what *not* to do. Just the thought of becoming like him sent chills through me. I avoided alcohol just in case I had inherited the "alcoholic gene" that my brother Stewart had talked about. Even though Stewart had sworn he would never become an alcoholic, somehow he had. I didn't want that to happen to me. I often carried around a drink at social gatherings, pretending to join in the fun, only to dump it into a plant or down the sink late in the evening when no one was looking.

Patrick thought I was taking "not becoming an alcoholic" too far.

"If you were going to be an alcoholic, you'd be one by now," he insisted. "You are not your father." He wrapped his arms around my waist. "Come on," he whispered, "let me teach you how to drink. You're missing one of the finer things in life."

Fall had arrived, and along with the scattered leaves went the last shred of my good judgment. If Patrick wanted a partner who drank occasionally, well, I could do that too. And I'd be very careful not to fall into the same trap my brother Stewart had.

Patrick and I drove my car over to his favorite haunt, 5th Street Bar, which distinguished itself from the antique shops and boutiques surrounding it by a neon Pabst Blue Ribbon sign blinking in the tinted window. We could hear the jukebox from the sidewalk: Elvis Presley's sultry voice sang "Are You Lonesome Tonight." We walked into the bar and a dozen patrons looked up from their drinks and checked us out from head to toe. The men looked at me, and the women looked at Patrick. As Patrick walked over to the bar, a thirtyish woman with curly blonde hair and too much makeup eyed him like a cat, kissed her lips together, and blinked slowly. Patrick ignored her, but as he sidled up to the bar, his posture changed. He went from a lost puppy in need of care to a cocky rogue. James Dean—delicate and dangerous. I slipped onto the stool beside him, giddy with excitement. As the music ended, Patrick nodded to the bartender. It seemed as if everyone in the joint listened to what he ordered.

"I'll have a shot of Jack Daniel's with a beer chaser," he said. "And the lady will have a shot with a Coca-Cola chaser." While the bartender got our drinks, Patrick walked over to the cigarette machine. As he walked, he pulled the rubber band from his ponytail, slicked his hair back with his palms, and snapped the rubber band around it again. He ran his hands over his black T-shirt and the hips of his jeans. Before he popped the money into the machine, he adjusted the vintage tooled-leather belt at his waist.

Even the men playing pool at the back of the room watched as Patrick sauntered back to the bar. He climbed onto his stool and asked the bartender for matches. He put a cigarette in his mouth, lit it, then wrapped his fingers around the shot glass, little finger jutting out—and there he was! My father: dark hair, green eyes, cigarette, and whiskey, emanating a sense of danger bordering on madness. I sucked in the smoky air, mesmerized by the familiarity of it, and exhaled as if I'd been holding my breath since the morning my dad died. I scanned the cigarette-burned countertop, half expecting to see my initials carved in the wood.

When I was a child, I carved my initials into several juke-joint countertops while waiting for my dad to trade his weekly paycheck for whiskey. He would sit at the bar and hold up his shot glass—little finger jutting out—certain the whiskey could put him in touch with God. He anticipated this weekly reunion with a fervor that spilled over onto me. I'd sit and watch him fade away like drifting smoke and imagine that if I could say or do the right thing, I could magically bring him back. When his chin nodded toward his chest, I'd ask to see his pocketknife, knowing that he would soon forget that I hadn't given it back. While the bartender was busy, I'd tool my initials into the soft wood.

I ran my hand across the bar now and looked up at Patrick. His resemblance to my dad was uncanny. Adrenaline rushed through me.

My eyes darted from Patrick's black T-shirt to mine; his jeans to mine. I felt like a female mirror image of him and hoped I looked half as beautiful. My hair was in a ponytail on top of my head, and dark curls cascaded around my face. I felt sexy, light-headed, and lucky to be with such a handsome man, thrilled that he had chosen *me*. And in a sense, he had. I had made the initial move, but was rejected. Patrick's words— "Who would want to take a bath with you anyway?"—had put me squarely in my place. When he'd jumped in the car to rescue me that night, even though he had caused the hurt, I was grateful. I sat at the bar with him and my heart raced. After a few minutes it eased into a strong, steady rhythm that pulsed in my fingertips against the hard surface of the shot glass.

"Drink it slow," Patrick said, nodding toward the whiskey. "Sip it. Then take a drink of cola." He took a sip of whiskey and then one of beer. "Like that. Otherwise, you'll be on your ass. You can sit here all night and never get drunk if you sip it." I did as he instructed. The whiskey burned in my chest as if I'd swallowed fire.

An old man with a long beard sat at the short end of the bar. He had looked me over when I'd first sat down, and now he was staring at me. He lifted his beer glass into the air. "You're a pretty thing," he said. "That boy better be careful. Somebody'll steal you away while he ain't looking." I blushed and smiled. Patrick blew smoke into the air. The old man looked at Patrick and said, "I ain't seen you in here in a while. Thought you mighta got throwed in jail."

"No," Patrick said, sipping his whiskey. "Just took a little break, that's all."

I sipped my whiskey, anticipating the warm rush it made in my chest, and watched Patrick in the mirror behind the bar. I studied his hands, the delicateness of them, the way they flicked ashes from his cigarette, rested on the bar. His fingernails were stained with oil paint, one fingernail lined in dark blue, another half red, half yellow. My hands had the same stains, but his were more beautiful than mine, smooth, flawless, like the hands in the Byzantine carving of Saint Michael the Archangel. I leaned on the bar and casually slid my hands next to his, letting the little finger of my right hand touch the little finger of his left, concentrating on the electricity that snapped from me to Patrick and back again through our touching fingers.

When my shot glass was empty, Patrick ordered us both another. By ten o'clock, I'd had three shots and Patrick had had four. Well, actually five, because he kept helping me with mine, picking up my shot glass and taking a sip, demonstrating the correct drinking technique.

After shooting the last sip of whiskey from number four, Patrick thumped the glass onto the bar and said, "I think we should go dancing." He turned and looked at me, his eyes sparkling with devilment.

Fire coursed through my veins. I giggled. We slid from the stools and ran to the car. I was dizzy and knew I shouldn't drive, but I wasn't about to let Patrick behind the wheel. I took the back roads to the downtown area, then followed Patrick's directions to the dance joint. The November air cleared my head a little. By the time we parked the car, I didn't feel dizzy anymore.

The dance joint had the front half of a pink Cadillac protruding out onto the sidewalk. A young man wearing a sleeveless shirt sat on a stool at the front door collecting cover charges. Huge muscles knotted his arms.

"The bouncer," Patrick said as we searched our pockets for money.

"I know," I said defensively. "I've been in plenty of bars before. I used to go all the time with my dad." I hiccuped, and the bouncer eyed me suspiciously.

"Five bucks apiece," he said. We emptied our pockets and came up with three dollars and eighteen cents.

"Damn," Patrick said. We stood in the cold staring at our money. Suddenly Patrick laughed and took off running. "I'm going to jump in the Des Moines River!" he shouted. I watched him run across the vacant lot across the street from the dance joint. I looked at the bouncer, and he shrugged. Patrick disappeared into the night, and I ran after him, laughing.

"Wait!" I yelled. "Wait for me!" I ran across the vacant lot. It was dark, but I saw Patrick jump onto the retaining wall next to the Des

Moines River Bridge a block away. I could hear the roar of the river over the pounding of my heart. The whiskey was rushing in my head. I slowed down. "Hey, wait for me!" I laughed, staggering closer.

Patrick laughed. "I'm gonna jump!" he shouted. I looked down at the ground to make sure my path was clear, held my chest, and breathed in the cold air. When I looked up again, Patrick was gone.

"Ha!" I shouted. I thought there must be a ledge just below the wall where he was hiding, waiting for me to approach so he could jump out and scare me. I inched toward the wall, anticipating the trick. But he didn't jump out at me. I looked over the wall, and there he was lying motionless, facedown, forty feet below on the ground. I thought he had somehow climbed down and was faking a fall. I leaned against the wall and laughed.

"Ha!" I shouted. "You're not scaring me! How did you get down there?" Patrick didn't answer. I gasped for air, wrapped my shirt tighter around me, and leaned farther over the wall.

"Patrick! You're not scaring me! Come on. It's freezing out here!"

Patrick moved just a little and moaned. I blinked, held my breath, and tried to focus. Patrick slowly rolled over, and blood trickled down his arm. Even from forty feet up and in the dark, I knew his arm was broken. "Jesus Christ," I whispered.

"Patrick!" I shouted. "Patrick, can you hear me!"

"Yeah." He said something else, but the roar of the river and the wind drowned it out.

"What?!" I shouted.

"My arm's broken!" he shouted back. "And maybe something else."

"Why'd you jump?!"

"I didn't jump!" He pushed himself up with his good arm. "I was just kidding, but I lost my balance!"

"I saw a police car two blocks back. I'm gonna go get them!"

"No!" Patrick screamed, sitting up. "No! Don't get the police! They'll arrest me for public intoxication!"

"Patrick, it's twenty degrees out here. You don't have on a coat and there's no way to get you back up!"

"I'll walk!" Patrick said, pushing himself up. "The retaining wall ends about six blocks down . . . and there's some stairs." He stood up, hunched over. His wrenched arm dripped with blood. He clutched it against his chest and staggered a few feet.

"Patrick! I'm going for the police!"

"No! I can make it! They'll put me in jail, Barbara! Please, don't leave me here!" He staggered forward, disappearing into the night.

"Patrick!" I shouted. "Patrick!" I could barely see him. I didn't know what to do. I was afraid he would go into shock before he made it to the staircase. I started to run for the police, then turned and ran along the retaining wall toward the stairs. Snowflakes hit my cheeks as I ran. *Please, God,* I prayed. *Don't let anything happen to him. I won't drink anymore. I won't do anything anymore.*

"Barbara!" Patrick cried.

"I'm here!"

He called again, and I answered, "I'm here! I'm right here! I can see you!" I ran along the bank, dodging brittle shrubs and tree limbs. I found a clearing and ran along the edge, panting, searching for Patrick in the dark. I could see him below, hunched over, holding his arm. I could see his labored breath in the cold night air, hear the noises forced from his broken chest like those from a cornered animal. Chills shook me. I looked back in the direction I had come, already snow-covered.

At last, I spotted the stairs and sprinted, making it there before Patrick, and rushed down them two at a time. He stumbled up, hunched into himself, gasping for breath. Blood dripped from his fingertips. I put my arm around his stone-cold shoulders, took his good arm, and lifted him up. He moaned, sucked in the cold air, and fell forward with each step. I thought he might faint. Shivering violently, we staggered the six blocks back, snow blinding our path. Finally we made it to the car and collapsed onto the seats.

Patrick didn't have medical insurance, so I drove him to the emergency room at Broadlawns, the county hospital. A nurse escorted us into a small room, eased Patrick onto the table, and washed the blood from his arm and hand. She bandaged his wounds, then took him for an X-ray. She brought him back a few minutes later and stuck the X-rays on the light box against the wall. She shook her head and said, "Well, you don't have to be a genius to find those."

The doctor, a young intern, ran his finger over the X-rays. "A fractured rib. But it's not bad. And a break here," he said, turning and pointing to Patrick's arm. "And here, and here, and here," he said, pointing to fingers. "We'll have to put you in traction for a little while before I can set them." He looked over at me. "And you'll have to wait outside."

I didn't want to wait outside. When we'd come through the waiting room, there was an angry biker screaming at everyone. I could still hear him through the closed door. Oblivious to the shouting, the doctor wrote on Patrick's chart and nodded for me to leave.

As soon as I closed the door behind me, the biker rushed toward me, hoping I would be the one person who would listen to him. He propped an arm against the wall beside my head and leaned over me.

"He shot my brother in the face!" he yelled. I closed my eyes, trembling as his stale-whiskey breath hit my face. When I opened them again, he had propped the other arm against the wall, blocking me in. Tattooed black widow spiders ran up both of his arms and circled his shoulder. "A fucking nigger shot my brother," he said, shaking his head, flinging his hair in my face. I shivered, ducked under his arm, and scooted away.

"Oh!" he shouted. "You don't give a damn neither! Is that it? He shot my brother in the face, but you don't give a damn!"

I pushed away from the wall and walked quickly toward the waiting room, hoping to lose him, but he followed on my heels. Suddenly the waiting room filled with his motorcycle gang buddies.

"Judd! Clifford! Hutch!" he shouted. They ran toward him as he continued to shout and point down the hall. "I think he's dead! That fuckin' nigger killed my brother!" The gang gathered around him. All of the men had black spiders on their arms, and the women, all bleached blondes, had six-inch round holes cut in the seats of their tight-fitting jeans and black widows tattooed on each butt cheek.

I leaned against the wall in the hallway and watched as the group divided, the men on one side, the women on the other, everybody talking at once.

Two police officers came into the waiting room, spotted the motor-cycle gang, and walked briskly toward them. The group fell silent. But the young man who had been yelling earlier began yelling again.

"He shot my brother!" He pointed down the hall where the injured man had been taken. "That fuckin' nigger walked right in the bar and shot my brother in the face with a shotgun!"

"Quiet down!" the larger of the officers said. The other held up a clipboard, pulled a pen from his breast pocket, and began to write.

"Name," he said.

"My name?" the biker asked.

"Your brother's name," the officer replied.

"Buster. His name's Buster."

"Last name?"

The biker stopped, as if out of breath. He looked at the floor, then back at the officer. "Well, I don't know what his last name is."

The officer looked up from the clipboard. "Didn't you say he was your brother?"

"Well, yeah."

"So what's his last name?"

"I dunno."

"If he's your brother, isn't it the same as yours?" the officer asked, annoyed.

"Naw, man. He's my brother, but he didn't have the same last name."

"Well, what *is* his last name?"

"I dunno, man."

The officer looked at the biker reproachfully. "He's your brother, but you don't know his last name?" The officer paused for a minute, glanced at the other officer, then went back to the clipboard. "Does *anybody* here know his last name?"

The group mumbled, but no one knew. The officer sighed, lowered his clipboard, and glanced over at me. I was suddenly aware of how I must look: half-frozen, half-drunk, mouth hanging open in shock. I remembered what Patrick had said about being arrested for public intoxication. I closed my mouth and dropped my gaze, hoping to look inconspicuous. When the officer turned his attention back to the motorcycle gang, I slipped back into the room with Patrick and the doctor.

"I can't stay out there," I explained to the doctor as I shut the door. "I'm too scared to stay out there." The intern nodded as I made my way to Patrick. He lay on a table with his arm and three fingers suspended in wire mesh pulled tight with weights. His bare rib cage was taped and packed in ice. He looked up, smiled, and reached for me with his good arm.

"She's my guardian angel," he said as he locked his fingers through mine. The intern looked at me, and we smiled at each other.

"She looks like she'd be a good one," the intern said, picking up a large needle from a tray. "I need to move the bones around in your wrist." He looked at me. "You're not squeamish, are you?"

"No. No, not at all." And I was telling the truth. When I had worked for a dentist who specialized in oral surgery, I had assisted with everything from extracting wisdom teeth to removing cancers on lips and tongues.

But when the intern pushed the huge needle into Patrick's wrist, I felt the blood drain from my face. I backed away from the table, out the door, and slid along the hallway until I came to another door. I opened it, praying the room would be empty, and collapsed to the floor.

Everything turned black with tiny flecks of dancing light. The room careened in a wide circle like a lopsided carnival ride, and sweat poured from my face, warming my frozen nose. My ears began to ring, drowning out even the commotion down the hall.

I prayed for the second time that night. *Please, God, don't let anyone come in here. Please, don't let anyone find me like this.* The room whirled around and around. All I could think about was the needle in Patrick's bruised and broken wrist. I'd seen blue and purple bruising like that before. When I was a teenager, my dad had been badly beaten by thugs. Most of his body had turned purple with deep, sickening bruises.

I lay there until the nausea lifted and the spinning slowed. The lights were off in the room, but light filtered in under the door. I could see shapes again and focused on them until they twirled out of sight:

window, curtain, sink, mirror, and trash can. I breathed slowly in and out, in and out.

As soon as I was able, I sat up and slid against the wall for support. *Thank you, God. Thank you for giving me time to recover.* I sat for another five minutes, slowly breathing, getting the strength back in my legs. My eyes adjusted to the dark, and I pushed myself up and made my way to the sink. I washed my face, dried it with a paper towel from the dispenser, and leaned forward to gaze in the mirror. I looked perfectly normal. Pale, but no one would be suspicious if they found me now. I pulled the rubber band from my hair and shook it out. Then I pulled out a lipstick from my pocket, drew long lines across both cheeks, rubbed the color in, and studied the image. I ran the lipstick over my bottom lip. As I smacked my lips together, I spotted a gurney behind me in the mirror. I stuffed the lipstick back into my pocket and turned around.

There, in the dark, was the biker who had been shot. Most definitely dead. His face was gone. Nothing left but a bowl-like skull filled with muck. I ran my hand over my own face, searching in the dark for nose, cheekbones, lips, and chin.

Like the man on the gurney, I had been without a face before. At least without *this* face, my face now. Where I grew up in the remote hills of Alabama, beetles and june bugs danced on the surface of the water pulled from the well, and the sicknesses caught from that water were treated with chicken soup and mustard plasters. Houses had rats, puppies had worms, and little girls went to bed hungry. And hunger grows crooked little girls. At least *I* grew crooked, my face did.

The opposite of the dead biker's spooned-out face, mine had been long and rocky, an unforgiving mountain range. The long upper jaw pushed the lower jaw back. All through my school years, the boys had taunted me.

"Hey, Bucktooth Beaver," Bob shouted in the lunchroom line. "Hey, you, Dog Face, do you want a bone?"

I presented my mother's taciturn stance and pretended not to hear him.

"Howl for us, Buckie, and I'll throw you a bone."

I turned ever so slightly so that I couldn't see his antics, but my blood ran hot. *I'll transform,* I told myself. *I'll transform into a beautiful woman, and I'll be a successful artist. You'll see.*

The taunting fueled a desperate desire in me to become someone who commanded respect—and got it. It drove me to pursue a beautiful face—and a beautiful life to go with it. I planned my transformation. I would have a fine profile; I would.

My face was a medical condition, as well as an aesthetic one, and the year before I ran away to art school, my doctor told me about an experimental procedure where the bones of the face could be cut through and reshaped. I drove to Birmingham and offered my face to the University of Alabama Hospital. The surgeon—as if excavating for a new highway—sliced my mountainous face in two, shortened and softened it, and slid the pieces back together. I was delighted with the results of the surgery: a heart-shaped face with fine features. Yet it took a long time for me to feel confident about this new face. I was used to seeing the old one, used to being passed over. It took years before I felt secure enough to kiss a man with pretty features, a man like Patrick.

So I kissed him, and kissed him, and poured my life into him, telling him all about my face surgery and the years of hurt and anger that had preceded it. I wanted him to understand; him with his perfect profile. The fall from the Des Moines River Bridge hadn't left a single scar on his beautiful face. His hands were no longer perfect, at least they weren't straight anymore; each finger on his left hand healed curly, like a lightning-struck tree. But the crooked fingers seemed only to add more charm to his character. And his face was still perfect, the most beautiful face I'd ever seen.

love notes

"Stewart's drinking again," Mother said over the phone. "It took a month to get him dried out and his face repaired. He scared us all to death. But he's right back at it. He makes it a few weeks, then starts again with a vengeance. And he's having seizures. I don't know if the seizures are triggered when he drinks or when he tries to *stop* drinking. I don't know what to do for him."

"Is he still going to AA?" I asked.

"Yes, but he's drinking between meetings." Mother paused. "I don't think he *can* quit. He wants to. He needs help, and I don't know how to give it to him."

Stewart's drinking upset me much more than my dad's ever had. Maybe because I hadn't known Dad before he started to drink, but I had known Stewart—and had known of his original conviction not to follow in Dad's footsteps.

I couldn't sleep that night. All I could think about was Stewart, and his drinking problem, and how I could possibly help him. I couldn't bear the thought of losing him. My nerves twitched just thinking about it.

The next day I went to see a doctor. I'd had a terrible stomachache for a long time, and that's what I talked to him about, but what I really wanted to know was more about a drug called Antabuse.

"Antabuse?" the doctor asked. "It's a drug that stops the breakdown of alcohol in your body. If you take it and drink, you'll get sick and vomit." He eyed me suspiciously. "Are you drinking?"

I didn't answer. I hadn't had a bit of alcohol since Patrick's "drinking lesson." That one night had scared the hell out of me. It wasn't likely I'd ever drink more than a sip again in my lifetime. But the doctor didn't know that. I kept quiet, thinking about how to answer him. I couldn't tell him I wanted a prescription for my brother, especially since he knew it would be paid for by my government insurance, Title XIX.

"Listen," he said. "I know you've got a lot going on right now. You're in school and trying to raise a child. But drinking isn't the answer to your problems. In fact, it might be why your stomach hurts so badly."

I looked up, surprised at his assumption, and almost told him that I didn't drink, but he pulled a prescription pad from his pocket, and I stopped myself.

The doctor scribbled on the pad. "I'm going to write you a prescription for Antabuse. You can decide whether to take it or not." He tore it off and waved it at me. "But you be careful. This stuff will make you plenty sick if you drink on top of it."

I took the prescription and had it filled at an out-of-the-way pharmacy. That night I wrote a note to Stewart.

Dear Stewart,
   This is Antabuse. It will make you throw up if you take it and drink. Please don't be mad at me.
                                        Love, Barbara

The next day, I put the note and the prescription in a small box and sent it to Stewart. I felt good about what I had done. Maybe Antabuse was something he hadn't tried. The next few days I daydreamed about his miraculous recovery.

Then the package came back—with a note from Stewart.

Dear Barbara,
   Take this Antabuse and use it as a suppository.
                                        Love, Stewart

making crazy

*E*very Christmas Eve, Mother threw a party. Jason and I flew home to Alabama, joining all of my brothers and sisters, and all of their children.

At Thanksgiving, Alice had officiated the annual drawing of names for Christmas gifts. This year, I was glad to have Doris Ann's name. I didn't have any money, but I had a beautiful pair of diamond earrings (relics from my marriage) that she had often admired. I promised them to her as a Christmas present if she'd pierce her ears. When I got into town before the party, I went by to see her. She smiled at me as I walked up the steps. Sure enough, she had little silver hoops in her lobes.

I dropped onto the porch swing. "You look great," I said. And she did. She was trim and curvy, her blond hair had grown out, and she was wearing pale pink lipstick.

"Thanks," she said, and sat next to me. "I'm starting my New Year's resolution early. I work like a dog all the time. I hardly ever have a reason to put on makeup or jewelry."

Inwardly, I winced at the mention of New Year's resolutions. The thought of another year like last year made me queasy. We sat in the swing and rocked back and forth without saying anything for a few minutes. Then Doris Ann pointed to the end of the house. "And I'm going to build a carport."

Doris Ann could handle power tools the way I handled hot rollers, and she'd just finished building the porch we were sitting on. A couple of years before, she had bought this old battered house and single-handedly torn out walls, built closets and an extra bedroom. Outside, she had added the porch, fenced in the yard, cut down trees, and planted grass. She'd turned a tumbledown house into a beautiful home. A jewel. I was amazed, and envious.

When we were kids, she was the one Mother called on when she needed *real* help. I could babysit and help cook. But Doris Ann could do anything, including swing a hammer like a carpenter.

Mother's Christmas Eve party was a smashing success. She cooked a turkey and several fancy desserts. After dinner we sang carols and opened presents. Doris Ann slipped the hoops from her ears and put in the diamond earrings. She walked around, showing them to everyone, and I blushed, grateful that I had had something nice to give her, even if it was a hand-me-down.

Early the next morning, Doris Ann and her fourteen-year-old daughter, Kelly, returned to Mother's house. I could tell by the way she sped into the yard that something was wrong. I met them on the porch.

Doris Ann was gasping for air and held one hand over her badly bruised neck. Tears streamed down her cheeks. "Harvey tried to kill me," she croaked. "He wrapped a belt around my neck and tried to choke me to death."

Mother came out onto the porch. "What? She saw Doris Ann's neck and said, "Good Lord." She put her arm around her and led her inside. Kelly followed and dropped into the rocking chair; Doris Ann collapsed on the couch with me on one side and Mother on the other. Mother patted Doris Ann's back. "What in the world is going on?"

Doris Ann's voice sounded as if she'd screamed herself hoarse. "He tried to kill me," she sobbed. "He said he'd kill Kelly too." Kelly nodded. Tears ran down her face.

Harvey, Doris Ann's husband, had seemed fine the night before. "What happened?" I asked.

"He had a fit about those earrings you gave me for Christmas,"

Doris Ann told me. "He said I was turning into a whore because I got my ears pierced."

Mother and I looked at each other. "That's ridiculous," Mother said, running her fingers over the fist-size bruises on Doris Ann's arms. Doris Ann put her face in her hands and sobbed.

Jason stumbled sleepily into the room and fell into a chair. "What's going on?"

Before I could say anything, Doris Ann said, "He started in on me as soon as we left the party last night. He said I'd lost weight and pierced my ears to attract other men." She struggled to get enough air in her lungs to continue. "I been gonna ask him for a divorce for a year. I'd made up my mind that after Christmas, that was it. I was gonna tell him that I was getting a divorce. But last night, he was so mean and god-awful, I told him as soon as we got in the door. I told him I hated him and wanted a divorce!" She cried into her hands again. "He's been such a rotten bastard. I hate his guts! He knocked me down and put that belt around my neck. He tightened it till I choked and screamed in my face." She looked over at Kelly. "You wouldn't believe the terrible things he said about Kelly!"

Kelly cried, "He called me a harlot, Grandma. A harlot. I don't even know what a harlot is."

Mother looked at Kelly and shook her head. "Don't pay any attention to that ol' fool, honey."

"He was going to kill us!" Doris Ann cried.

As if on cue, Jason and I both said, "How'd you get away?"

"His sister called. He got on the phone with her and told her he was gonna kill me, and she talked him into taking the belt off my neck. Then he sat down on the couch and started crying to his sister. Me and Kelly ran out the door."

The phone rang, and Doris Ann jumped to her feet. "That's him. I'll get it." She answered the phone, burst into tears, and hung it up again. "He says he's coming over here to kill me!" Her body shook so badly that Mother had to drag her back to the couch.

"He's gonna kill me," she cried.

"He's not gonna kill anybody," Mother said. "He just wants to scare you."

A few minutes later, Harvey drove past the house in his pickup truck and fired his pistol into the woods before driving on. I ran to the phone and called my brothers. Before we knew it, Willie and John appeared at Mother's house. They took one look at Doris Ann and decided Harvey had lost his mind and that we needed protection. John had an old pistol in the glove box of his truck, but he didn't want to kill anyone with that sorry old gun, so they all went back home to get their good guns.

While they were gone, Harvey called again. And once again Doris Ann answered and hung up in tears. She pointed to me. "He says he's going to kill us all, and that it's all your fault. He says it's your fault I pierced my ears."

"My fault!" I cried.

"Yeah, I wouldn't have pierced them if you hadn't promised me those diamonds. Now he's gonna kill us all."

"How was I supposed to know Harvey'd kill us over a pair of earrings?!"

Mother said, "All right, that's enough." We all fell silent for a moment.

I said, "I think we should call the police."

"And what will they do?" Doris Ann cried. "You're always in more trouble with them than without them!"

Doris Ann was right. Down South, it's common knowledge that if you aren't rich, the police are of no help, but I had been living up North long enough to forget that. Harvey called again, repeating his threat, and I called the police. I told them what had been going on, and they said they would drive over to Harvey's house and tell him to knock it off. When I hung up the phone, Doris Ann was mad at me.

"Barbara, you overreact to everything!"

"Harvey's threatening to kill us, and I'm overreacting?!"

"The police are gonna go over there and turn this into a big mess."

"Harvey's gonna kill us and that's not a big mess?!"

Mother said, "That's enough," and we stopped bickering.

Willie and John came back with enough firearms to start a war. John had a carrying case with two Taurus 9mm automatics, complete with extra clips and enough ammunition to shoot down a pine tree—

and just in case that wasn't enough, an Army .45. Willie waved a beat-up .357 Magnum that hadn't been fired in years. They moved Mom's end tables out of the way and set up their post in front of the windows facing the road.

John said, "He better not come back by here, if he knows what's good for him."

Willie said, "We don't want to hurt him, though."

John said, "The hell I don't. If he shoots at me, I'll cap the mutherfucker."

Jason said, "Where's Stewart?"

The boys stood in front of the windows and talked about their guns, and Mother made everybody a cup of hot tea. In between Harvey's phone calls, my sisters-in-law called, demanding that their husbands come home. After all, it was Christmas morning and couldn't we fight tomorrow?

An hour went by, and Harvey didn't call or show up to kill us. Mother sent the boys back to their wives.

Doris Ann paced the floor for a while, going over in detail everything that had happened the night before. She managed to work herself into a lather and finally called home to yell at Harvey. When he didn't answer, she said, "I'm going to get my stuff."

"What?" I said. "Are you crazy?!"

"He's not home. And I'm not leaving my stuff over there." She looked around for her car keys. "He's already torn the pictures out of my photo albums and smashed my best iced-tea glasses."

Mother said, "I don't think you should go back over there." But she didn't say it with conviction. Mother wasn't much for putting her foot down.

"I'm going," Doris Ann said. "That son of a bitch better not a smashed any more of my stuff."

Doris Ann drove away while Mother, Kelly, Jason, and I stood on the porch watching her go. I was afraid I'd never see her alive again. My stomach hurt and my whole body trembled. I listened until the sound of Doris Ann's car died away, then sat down on the steps and began to rock back and forth. Little white spots floated in front of my eyes, and I thought I might be sick. It was the same sensation I had

had when Dad had committed suicide. And it felt to me like Doris Ann was about to commit suicide. But she drove away as if she were completely blind to the possibility of danger. Kelly sat down beside me and started to cry all over again. I put my arm around her and told her everything would be all right. But I didn't expect it to be.

I wanted to run away. Go back to Iowa, where I thought it was safe. For a brief moment, the crazy things that Patrick did seemed like a cakewalk.

Doris Ann made it back, but just barely. Harvey had driven up while she was packing her things. He chased her out the back door, and she took off through the woods, slapping through branches until she came out on the other side by the filling station at the bottom of the hill. The station attendant drove her to Mother's house.

We all stood on the porch and watched her climb out of the car. She was bleeding from a dozen places where tree branches had whipped her as she escaped through the woods.

Mother shook her head and said, "For crying out loud."

Doris Ann was livid. "That rotten, rotten bastard!"

Mother dragged her back to the couch and got a washcloth and ointment. While she was doctoring cuts, the phone rang again. Doris Ann tried to get up, but Mother pushed her back down. She tossed the washcloth onto the floor and stomped to the phone. "You listen to me!" she yelled into the receiver. "If you harm my daughter, I'll kill you myself! Do you hear? *I* will kill you! Now you stop this nonsense right this minute, and don't you dare call here again." She slammed the receiver into the cradle, and we all stared in astonishment. We'd seldom heard our mother yell. Jason and I smiled at each other.

A few minutes went by, and the phone rang again. Doris Ann looked at Mother, but Mother was exasperated and shrugged. Doris Ann answered the phone, talked for a minute, and hung up.

"That was Harvey," she said. "The police were on their way over to my house and stopped Stewart down at the bottom of the hill. He's drunk. They just took him to jail." She shot me that *I told you so* look.

My heart dropped to my stomach. Mother didn't say anything, but I could feel the blame float in my direction.

John walked in the door and announced, "Stewart's in jail. Driving while intoxicated."

"Yeah, we know," Doris Ann said. "Harvey just called. He said he'd bail him out if I'd go up there with him."

"That's crazy!" John yelled. "You're not gonna go with him?"

I said, "What's gonna keep him from killing you once you get in the truck?"

Doris Ann looked at us like we'd lost our minds.

John said to Mother and me, "Can't we bail him out?"

Doris Ann said, "You have to own property. It has to be either me or Alice. We're the only ones that own property."

John looked at me. I shrugged. "I don't own anything, and Alice has gone to her in-laws'."

Mother sighed and dropped into the rocking chair.

Just then Harvey pulled into the yard and honked his horn. Doris Ann walked out the door as if nothing had happened and climbed in the cab of his truck.

The next day Jason and I flew back to Iowa. The trip had been frightening and exhausting, but beyond that, it left my thinking befuddled: I considered the antics in Alabama against Patrick's unsound behavior and thought they were the same thing. I told myself, *Patrick's crazy-making isn't different from anybody else's.*

how do you raise a boy?

*B*y the time Jason was sixteen, he was six feet tall and weighed 180 pounds and was quite rebellious. He was quick to stand up for his rights—even when they weren't being infringed upon. When I tried to control his behavior, even simple things like wearing a coat in freezing weather, he'd react with fierce indignation. I learned to pick my battles. A messy room I could tolerate. No jacket when it was ten degrees outside was a little harder to let slide. Drinking and driving was forbidden, and worth fighting over.

To my knowledge, Jason and his friends didn't drink that much. They were varsity basketball players and their coach prohibited drinking. Of course, that made them feel it was imperative. At some point I recognized they were *going* to drink, and it scared the hell out of me. What if Jason drank too much, and continued to drink more and more? What if, by rebelling against the "no drinking" rule established by his coach, he lost his way and succumbed to alcoholism?

Years earlier when my brother Stewart had asked me if I was watching Jason for signs of alcoholism, I had said yes, but it was easy then. Jason was still a boy. But now, when I looked at my man-child, I knew that anything I asked of him had to be reasonable, and that he would do it, not because I could make him do it (I couldn't, he was too big, too strong), but out of respect for his mother.

I decided to take a stand: all Jason's drinking (beer only, and I wouldn't buy a single bottle of it) would be done at home—where I could keep a furtive yet close watch on how much he drank. Since he

only drank at parties, the rule really meant that all parties had to be thrown at our house. The rules extended to guests: excessive drinking was prohibited, and anyone who did drink would have to spend the night or catch a ride home with a nondrinking friend.

Jason threw two or three parties a year. Most of them were just for the guys: Jason, Chris, Matt, Ken, and Budd. They'd bring in a couple of six-packs and cigars and play poker until three in the morning. I'd check on them every hour until they'd toss the cards aside and curl up on the couch and the floor to sleep. Occasionally, their girlfriends came along to watch the card games and smoke cigars. That was Jason's average party.

One Saturday night during his senior year, after a big 70–58 win for Hoover High School, Jason invited several of his teammates over to celebrate. He expected ten guys to show up, but the entire team came, and they brought their girlfriends. And their girlfriends' best girlfriends. And their cousins. The house was packed. Cars lined the street all the way around the circle drive and down several blocks. At 10 P.M., I came halfway down the stairs and tried to count heads: sixty-three kids! I spotted Jason talking to his girlfriend, Amanda, and shouted over the music and noise to get his attention. He looked up and shoved his way toward the stairs. "I've got it under control," he said. He looked around, smiled at me, and said, "I think."

I sat down on the steps, astonished. Jason's high school experience was so unlike mine. I had hoped simply that he would go through school with a few good friends, and that he wouldn't be tortured too much. Through the years I'd made sure he had good clothes, lunch money, sports fees, and medical care. I'd hoped for normal; I never dreamed he would grow so tall and beautiful, athletic and confident.

By 11 P.M., the house was packed, and our next-door neighbor called the police. Apparently one of the kids had parked his car in front of the neighbor's driveway. A policeman knocked, and one of the boys on the ball team answered the door. When he saw the uniform, he slammed the door and locked it. Jason had to wade through the crowd and let the officer in. The policeman asked if an adult was in the house, and Jason sent Amanda to get me out of bed.

The officer pointed at me as I descended the stairs and said, "You need to come with me." I was wearing a T-shirt, sweatpants, and fluffy socks.

"Can I get my shoes?" I asked.

"No," the officer said.

I looked out the window at the snow on the ground and ran up the stairs to get my tennis shoes and a hooded sweatshirt. When I returned, the officer took my arm and escorted me to the patrol car. He tucked me into the backseat and climbed into the front. His partner was sitting in the driver's seat with the engine running and the lights flashing, jotting down license plate numbers from the cars around our circle drive.

The officer who had escorted me to the car looked over his shoulder at me and said, "Ma'am, do you know that I can arrest you for contributing to the delinquency of minors?"

"Yes, sir."

"Then what in the world are you doing? You've got a hundred half-drunk kids in your house."

"They're *not* half-drunk. And if they weren't here, they'd be drinking in some bar or ripping up and down the road in their cars."

The officer shook his head. "They can't get into the bars."

"They get into the bars all the time."

He shook his head. "Ma'am, that's not good enough."

I sat up straighter and fidgeted. "Listen, I know my son. He's *going* to drink. And so are his friends. And I'm not willing to chance losing a single one of them in a car wreck. As long as they're drinking *here*, I know they're safe."

The officer said, "What about when they leave? You've allowed them to drink in your home, and later on they're gonna be *rippin' up and down the road*—half-drunk!"

I leaned forward. "Some of them are spending the night. And there are designated drivers for anyone who needs to get home. It's a house rule."

"A house rule," the officer mocked. "You've got designated drivers for every kid that has to go home?"

I nodded.

"Let's go," he said. He helped me out of the car and walked me back to the house. It was quiet. The music and the lights had been turned off so the kids could watch what was happening outside. When we walked in the front door, seventy-five stricken faces turned and stared. They were crowded into the living room with their arms crossed in front of their chests like prisoners in a cell. I flipped on the lights, and they blinked.

"How many of you are spending the night here?" the officer asked.

About twenty kids slowly raised their hands.

The policeman looked at me. "Not even half." He put his hands on his hips. "And how many of you are designated drivers?"

About fifteen kids raised their hands. The policeman shook his head. "Still not gonna make it," he mumbled.

"You," he said, pointing to a dark-haired girl I'd never seen before. "How much have you had to drink?"

The girl blushed and squeezed her arms around her chest. "Maybe two beers."

"Two beers?"

"Yes, sir."

"And you're staying here tonight?"

"No, sir."

"You riding with one of these designated drivers?"

The girl looked around. "No, sir. My sister's here. I'm riding with her." She looked frantically for her sister.

Another dark-haired girl pushed through the crowd and said, "I'm here, Brittany." She put her arms around her sister.

The officer clicked his tongue. He waved his hand over the crowd of kids and looked at me. "How you gonna keep all these kids from driving home?"

"I've got their keys." I dashed up the stairs. I came back with an Easter basket filled with car keys and held them out for the officer to see. "They can't get them back if they've been drinking."

The officer took a set of keys and held them up. "Whose are these? Nineteen eighty-six Honda Civic."

Jason's friend Budd held up his hand. "They're mine."

The officer nodded. "Your parents know where you are?"

"Not exactly. They know I'm out with the guys."

"They know you're drinking?"

He shrugged. "I don't know. Probably."

"If I call them and tell them, what will they do?"

Budd shrugged again. "Probably ground me and tell me I'm not allowed to drink ever again."

The officer nodded. "And would it work?"

Budd dropped his head and laughed. "No, sir." He caught the officer's expression and stopped laughing, cleared his throat, and straightened a little. But he didn't take it back.

The officer put the basket of keys on the stairs and addressed the crowd. "All right. I want these cars cleared out of here. I want every one of you to get on home."

As the kids began to pull on their coats and dig through the basket for keys, I was escorted back to the patrol car. As I climbed into the backseat, the officer behind the wheel sighed and crossed his arms over his chest as if to sleep awhile longer. The other officer climbed back into the front seat and looked over his shoulder and threatened to arrest me again.

"Do you think those kids are going home?" I asked. "It's just eleven-thirty."

"Those kids aren't your responsibility," the officer said.

"No, just *one* of them is. And if he's going to drink, he's going to drink where I can keep an eye on him. And if that comes with fifty other kids . . . well, so be it."

The officer leaned over the seat and shouted, "Most of those kids wouldn't be drinking if you didn't give them a place to drink!"

I leaned forward and shouted back, "You don't believe that for a minute!" We both fell back against our car seats.

A few seconds passed, and the officer spoke again. "I want you to promise me you won't let them drink here anymore."

"I won't do it."

"I won't arrest you if you promise. . . ."

"I won't. If they're here, they don't drink nearly as much because they know I'll be down to check on them. And they stay put— they're not on the road."

We sat in that patrol car and watched the kids drive away. Jason had told me stories of his friends drinking until they passed out, but they never behaved that way when they were at my house. They knew better than to drink too much, or to attempt driving. I'd told them repeatedly what I expected of them, and they had never let me down. On more than one occasion, Jason had called me at midnight to pick him and a few friends up from a bar they'd sneaked into. And that was okay too. I'd told them all, I'll come and get you, or I'll pay for a taxi—but never, never drink and drive.

Eventually the officer sitting behind the wheel got antsy and sat up. He shut off the ignition and turned to his partner. "It's not like that boy's throwing wild parties every weekend," he said. "We've never been called to this address before." He tapped his fingers on the wheel for a few seconds, then got out of the car and opened the back door.

I climbed out. "I can go?"

The officer nodded. "Thanks." I started toward the house, then stopped and looked at the officer who had let me out of the car. "I'm watching 'em."

He touched the bill of his hat and said, "I know you are."

basketball dreams

*S*ince we'd moved to Iowa, I'd been attending all of Jason's basketball games. I always sat on the third row behind the players' bench so I could hear the coach, the cheerleaders, and the students. When Jason made a basket and the students cheered his name, it was a thrill. Somehow, the universe had given my child athletic ability. It was the biggest surprise of my life. And I'd given it a lot of thought.

When we were growing up, none of us kids got to play sports, not even my brothers. We never had the money for them to participate. But maybe they had talents that were never realized. Or maybe Jason got his ability from his father. He certainly favored the man physically: tall, strong, blond hair, blue eyes. He didn't resemble me at all. If he didn't have an expression that's exactly like my mother's, exactly like my brother John's, I'd worry that they gave me the wrong baby at the hospital.

When Jason was little, four, five, six years old, I thought he was going to be like me. I loved the arts: painting, music, theater. I was a member of the community theater, and Jason often went to rehearsal with me. Like a sponge, he soaked up every word of every play we performed. He'd memorize the entire play. Shortly after Jason started first grade, he performed the overture to *Man of La Mancha* for his class. His teacher, delighted by the performance, called me at home and wanted to know where he got this talent. "From me," I told her. He didn't look like me, but he loved the things I loved. For a while.

Jason always talked about what he wanted to be when he grew up, and it changed from year to year: a fireman, a policeman, an actor. But I was as surprised as could be when his true love turned out to be *basketball.*

The Boys Club in Sarasota, Florida, had been ideal for basketball dreams. Most of the kids that played there were from the inner city. They didn't go to the Boys Club because they needed after-school care, they went to play ball. Jason was only eight years old when he first started going there after school. One day I came in to check on him just as four or five big guys trampled him in a rush to score.

"Don't kill him!" I yelled. The game stopped and they looked at me. One of the boys, he must have been about sixteen, picked Jason up and tossed him in the air as if he weighed nothing at all.

"He's all right," he said. "You can't kill this one. We've tried." He smiled at me, and then laughed out loud when Jason landed on his feet. He pointed at him and said, "See?"

By the time Jason got to high school, he easily made it onto the varsity basketball team. I'd never been to a basketball game before, or any sports event, for that matter. High school had been a horrible experience for me, and even if I'd had the money to go to a game and could have found a ride, the kids at the game would have tortured me because I was ugly and poor.

Years had gone by and I wasn't that girl anymore. Most of the time I didn't know who I was. I felt like I was sitting on a fence watching life pass by in two worlds—and I didn't belong on either side of that fence. But when I attended Jason's basketball games, I felt almost normal—safe and happy. Jason was on the court, and he was safe and happy too—which had been, since the day he was born, my greatest goal. I watched his games with a sense of satisfaction that I didn't have about anything else—and I never missed a game. One time, I had the flu something awful, but I went anyway. I wrapped a blanket around my shoulders, drove across the high school's manicured lawn, parked at the front entrance, and stumbled up the bleachers to the top rung. About halftime, I thought I might die. Still, it was worth it to watch Jason play. As with all of his games, I watched—and prayed, knowing always that a fine line separated us and disaster.

madman

That spring, Patrick's Navane prescription ran out. I called his doctor, but she hadn't seen him for more than a year and refused to renew the prescription unless he came to the office for a checkup. I made up reasons why he couldn't come in, then explained that I had taken responsibility for giving him his medication. (I didn't tell her I had been sneaking it into his food.) But she wouldn't compromise, and neither would Patrick.

"I can't make art when I take that stuff," he complained. "It makes me fat, it makes me lethargic, and creativity goes right out the window!"

He wasn't fat, and he wasn't lethargic, and his drawings were tacked on every inch of wall space throughout the house. I didn't know what to say. I considered telling him I'd been sneaking Navane into his grits, but I didn't want to say anything that might make him take his love away, so I just watched him work for a few minutes.

He was making a small collage with torn pieces of colored foil and oil paint. I hoped it would be mine. I felt desperate to hang on to Patrick, which could only happen if he stayed on his medication. I fantasized about sneaking into the hospital and stealing Navane for him, or stealing a prescription pad and writing it myself. Anything to keep him well, to keep him with me.

Before Social Services allotted me Title XIX insurance, I'd get medicines in creative ways. I simply couldn't afford to be sick. So whenever Jason or I had to see a doctor, usually for strep throat, I'd call the doctor's office the next day and tell them I needed to have another pre-scription called in.

"I accidentally knocked the bottle of antibiotic into the toilet," I'd lie.

The doctor would call another prescription in to the pharmacy, and I'd get it filled and hold on to it until one of us ran a fever or suffered with a sore throat. That way I saved the expense of an office visit.

I had tried to fill Patrick's prescription that way, but it had already expired. I thought about the prescription for Antabuse that I'd sent to Stewart. But I wasn't about to convince my doctor that I was not only an alcoholic *but also schizophrenic.*

A few weeks after the Navane ran out, the effects of the medicine wore off and Patrick started staring off into space again. His mood changed as quickly as the closing of a door. Things that he used to love, he now said he hated. He claimed that rock music, movies, and even the art he made were evil. All of this evil came from Satan. Satan pursued him, made him itch, and made him think about harming peo-ple he loved. He cut off his shoulder-length hair and started carrying my Bible around to protect him from evil spirits.

"That man is Satan," Patrick said, staring intently at a TV com-mercial.

"That is not Satan," I said.

Patrick pointed to the TV set, wide-eyed, and shouted, "God just called him Satan!"

"It's a commercial, Patrick."

"He's Satan! He's Satan! Oh, my God! I've got to do something!"

The next day we were standing in the yard when an airplane flew over.

"They're here!" he shouted, running for the house. "They're com-ing to steal my kidneys!"

I ran after him. "It's all right," I cried. "It's just an airplane." Patrick pulled me inside and flipped off the lights. "Shh," he whispered. "It's aliens. They're looking for me."

One day he would seem perfectly normal: go to work, come home, help me with supper, and talk to Jason about school. The next day he'd skip work and wander around town picking up crumpled cigarette packs, lollipop wrappers, bottle caps, and lost mittens. He drew countless portraits of me, only to tear them up and stuff them in the trash in a rage about how women brought sin to man. To prove to him that he wouldn't lose himself on medication, I confessed to having sneaked the Navane into his food, but he still refused to see his doctor.

"They'll lock me up again, Angel," he said. He had been calling me Angel since he'd fallen from the Des Moines River Bridge. I had saved his life, he claimed, and I was his guardian angel.

"Just let me stay here with you," he said. "As long as I have my guardian angel, I'll be fine."

I loved the idea of having saved his life and being his guardian angel. Despite everything I now knew about schizophrenia, I somehow convinced myself that Patrick's psychosis stemmed from a lack of love. I also decided that I could make up for what he hadn't gotten, and that he would blossom under the warmth of my unconditional love. I wasn't receiving unconditional love from him—but that would change, I told myself. As soon as he realized just how much I cared about him, he'd reciprocate.

Shortly after I arrived home one evening, Jason called and asked if he could spend the night with a friend. I told him it was all right, hung up the phone, and went to look for Patrick. I found him pulling weeds in our garden and bent down to get a glimpse of his face. I could usually tell how far gone he was by his eyes—bruised circles underneath usually meant that he would soon be staring into space or ranting. If his pupils were huge and frozen, there was a chance that he'd hallucinate—receive TV messages from aliens or believe spots on the tablecloth were signs of impending doom. His eyes were clear, but the circles underneath looked like overripe plums.

"Hey," I said. "Jason's going to spend the night with Budd, so it's just you and me."

Patrick stood up, kissed me on the lips, and smiled. "Sounds good."

I counted his smile as a good sign and wrapped my arms around him. We walked back to the house. At the back door, I noticed that the large sunflowers Patrick and I had planted by the kitchen window looked trampled.

"Jason has been crawling in this window again," I complained, propping up a huge blossom. "He must have lost his key. Looks like he trampled some of our sunflowers. I've told him not to climb in like that."

Patrick examined the flowers, and I went into the kitchen and called Jason.

"The flowers were already like that, Mom," Jason said. "I think I trampled them last month when they were smaller and they just grew crooked. I noticed them yesterday. Look at how twisted the stems are. I haven't broken in that window since you told me not to."

We talked a little while longer, then I hung up the phone and went out to find Patrick. In the few minutes I was on the phone, he had made a noose out of a long white rope; dangling from the noose was a board, about two feet long. Patrick had hooked the noose over the screen door and weaved the rope in and out among the sunflowers. I caught the swinging board and held it up. Jason's name had been written across it with a black Magic Marker. The hair on the back of my neck stood up.

"What is this?" I asked.

"It's a sculpture," Patrick replied sarcastically.

"That's not funny." I slid the board from the noose and clutched it to my chest. Patrick marched past me and slammed into the house.

"It wasn't meant to be funny," he said. I followed him inside, propped the board against the wall, and sat at the table watching as he began to wash the dishes. He put too much dishwashing liquid in the sink, and the bubbles swelled over the rim with the force of the hot water.

"Do you not like Jason?" I asked.

Patrick threw his hands into the air, flinging suds everywhere. "I hate the little son of a bitch!" he cried. "He is the most worthless person I've ever known! He lies and cheats at school and screams at teachers, mooches money from you, uses me as a taxi. He abuses his girlfriend and walks all over his friends. He doesn't appreciate anything. He doesn't do his part of the housework, and what he does do, he does half-assed!" Patrick took a deep breath, put his hands on his hips, and bent down so that he was face-to-face with me. "You need to know that your son has a problem. That boy emulates his so-called father. He lies, cheats, takes advantage of women, and even makes comments about the nudes that I've drawn as if they were pornography. His room is a wreck. He has no respect for me, or you, or himself. He doesn't care that we've tried to make it nice around here. He's sick, and you'd better realize that!"

"He's a teenager!" I cried, getting up from the table. "He's supposed to be awful."

"He's no damn good, Barbara! He has no respect for anyone!"

Weary, and anxious to have this argument over, I opened the cabinet and took out two china plates and several bowls. I put the dishes on the table and tried to hug him. He pushed me away and screamed, "No! You listen to me! You've got to listen to me! You've got a problem here!"

"He's a normal, awful teenager," I said, laughing nervously.

Patrick grabbed one of the china plates and threw it against the wall. It smashed and flew around the room, ricocheting off the table and cabinets. Adrenaline shot through me, and a chill ran down my spine. I tried to run, but Patrick caught my arm and pushed me against the sink.

"Your son is no good. He's selling crack and living on the street, and you can't even feel anything!"

I eased against the sink and tried to calm down. After years of single parenting, Jason and I were close. I knew him well. He did just enough schoolwork to stay on the basketball team, and he never missed a practice or game. On Saturday nights, if he didn't have a game, he went out with his long-standing girlfriend, and he always made it home before his 11 P.M. curfew. Granted, Jason was occasionally disrespectful, but he was a normal teenager.

"What are you talking about, Patrick? Selling crack and living on the street? What are you talking about?"

Patrick grabbed my shoulders. "You can't feel a thing, can you?" He shook me, snapping my head back and forth. "Your ex-husband fucked everybody in town. How does that make you feel?"

I opened my mouth to protest, but Patrick cut me off.

"The son of a bitch was fucking his secretary!" Patrick pulled me from in front of the sink and slammed me against the wall. I struggled to get free, but he pressed his body against mine.

I shouted, "Let go of me!"

"No! You're gonna listen to me! Your ex-husband fucked all your friends!"

"He did not."

"He did!"

Hysterical laughter rolled from my chest like the cry of a cat. Patrick pulled me forward and slammed me into the wall again.

He screamed in my face, "What was the name of the woman your husband was fucking in the hotel while his friend and her husband watched? Tell me that! What was her name?"

"I don't know what you're talking about!" I screamed back.

"Why don't you know?! What was the name of the friend?!"

"Let go of me, please!"

Patrick shoved me away. He put his hands on his hips and breathed hard; sweat ran down the side of his face and he wiped it away with his shoulder. He looked at me with disgust, kicked at a shard of the broken plate, then turned and walked out of the kitchen and stomped up the stairs. I dropped onto a kitchen chair. Pain shot through my stomach, and my knees shook. I took long, deep breaths, trying desperately to get control of the strange laughter that whistled from my chest. My knees shook against the table leg, rattling the plate and the stack of bowls. I put my hands on my knees to stop the trembling so I could listen to what was happening upstairs. Doors and dressers opened and closed. I was afraid my hysterical laughter would return, so I sat at the table, as still as possible, listening to the movement upstairs. Patrick was packing his clothes.

He's leaving me. He's leaving me, and I'll be alone again. I shouldn't have said anything about the goddamn flowers! Why did I have to open my mouth? I know Patrick is jealous of Jason. Why did I say anything? It was so stupid of me. I shouldn't have said anything. He's leaving.

He won't leave. Doesn't have anywhere to go. He'll wind up living on the street again. He'll go crazy again. I'll go crazy. . . .

Finally, the fear of losing Patrick was greater than the fear of what he might do to me, and I climbed the stairs. I inched into the room and looked around. Nothing had been packed. Patrick had been opening and closing the drawers to draw me upstairs. He took my arm and pulled me to him. We sat on the bed for a while, catching our breath. When I thought the episode had passed, I put my hand on his and spoke in my most soothing voice.

"Patrick, I realize Jason has been difficult, but he *is* a normal teenager."

Patrick jerked his hand from mind. "He's spoiled!" he shouted. "He's worthless! He has no integrity whatsoever!" He jumped up, raced across the hall, and threw open Jason's bedroom door. "Look at this room!" he shouted. "He obviously has no self-respect at all. Look at these walls, crammed full of low-life scum!"

I leaned into the bedroom and looked around at the posters on the walls: three basketball players, four rap singers, and a black-and-white Marilyn Monroe with her dress billowing around her thighs.

I pointed to a poster of a basketball player. "Patrick, those people contribute a lot to society."

"Contribute what?!" Patrick yelled, cutting me off.

"They're famous basketball players and musicians."

"That's bullshit! The important word is *famous*." Patrick made quotations in the air with both hands. He breathed hard, put his hands on his hips again, and leaned toward me. "You just don't want to admit that you can't control your psychotic son. You're a bad mother and you've blocked it out so you can't feel anything anymore." He took a step toward me, and I could feel his breath on my face. "Just a bad mother that can't control her psychotic son."

My neck tightened into a hard knot, and the hair at the nape stood on end. I looked at the floor and didn't speak. I thought about trying to get away from him, but he stood between the stairway and me. I'd never get by. Patrick straightened and panted for a few seconds, then took one step forward, closing the space between us. When he spoke again, it was a whisper.

"Your father shot himself in the head. How does that make you feel?"

The whistle in my chest turned into a strange growl.

"How does that make you feel?!" he screamed. I put my hands over my ears and closed my eyes. The growling in my chest grew louder, a hoarse retching noise. Pressing my hands more firmly over my ears, I tried to block out the sound of Patrick's voice and my own.

"You think it's funny?!" He grabbed my wrists, threw me to the floor, and straddled me, pinning my wrists on either side of my head. "How does that make you feel?!"

I tried to push him off.

"Open your eyes!" he demanded. I opened them and began to cry. The strange growling became a hysterical mixture of laughing and crying. Patrick leaned his face toward mine and said, "You've got to face it: you've got a problem and so does your psychotic son."

I shook my head and the strange growling noise in my chest grew louder.

"You think it's funny!" he shouted. "All your life everyone has abused you—from your father, your child, your husbands, even your mother couldn't give you what you needed! The only person who has ever given you anything is *me*!"

I wrenched my arms and legs, trying to push him off me.

"Go ahead and struggle; you can't get free. I've finally got my hands on you, after all these years."

I stopped struggling and looked in his eyes. Adrenaline shot through me again. I shouted, "Get off of me, Patrick!"

"No."

"What makes you any better than anyone else who has abused me?!" I cried. "I'm being held against my will and you're screaming in my face!"

"This is for your own good. You have got to wake up and stop drifting off into space. Listen to me. You've got to realize that your son is sick and needs help. He needs help, and I can help him."

I didn't know what to do. My arms hurt from struggling. I relaxed, hoping he would loosen his grip. "I'll listen," I promised. "Just let me go to the bathroom. I'll come right back."

"No," Patrick said. I closed my eyes. He screamed, "Don't fade away! You've got to stop drifting off! You've got to wake up. Do you realize that your father blew his brains out?! How does that make you feel?!"

Patrick loosened his grip. I yelled, "Get off me," pulled free, and tried to punch him in the face, but he caught my wrist again. I shouted, "Let me go!"

"No! You've got to listen. Your father took a gun and blew his fuckin' brains out, Barbara! How does that feel? He took a gun and blew his fuckin' brains out!" Patrick pulled my wrists down, tucked them under his thighs, and squeezed his legs together to hold them there. With his left hand, he made a gun shape, held his index finger to his temple, and pretended to shoot himself, dropping his thumb as he fired.

"Pow!" he shouted. He pulled the trigger again. "Pow!" I closed my eyes.

"What do you think it feels like to have a bullet hit you in the head? Your father blew his fuckin' brains out!" Patrick shot himself with the imaginary gun again and slapped himself on the cheek with his right hand. "Pow! It must feel like that. Don't you think? Pow!" Patrick slapped himself again. "Pow!" and slap. "Pow!" and slap. "Pow!" and slap. He slapped himself over and over, each time striking harder. Sweat fell from his face onto mine. He was getting dizzy. I freed one of my hands and tried to wipe his stinging sweat from my eyes, but Patrick grabbed my hand and stuffed it back under his leg.

"Don't try that again!" he screamed in my face. "Pow! Your father blew his fuckin' brains out! Pow!" and he slapped himself again. I was afraid that he was going to stop slapping himself and start slapping me. I was afraid he was going to kill me. I started to cry hysterically.

"Mom!" I cried. "Mom!" I cried for my mother, who was a thousand miles away in Alabama. I fought to get free with all my might. "Who do you think you are?!" I yelled. "Get off me!"

Patrick had to use both hands to hold me down, so he couldn't slap himself anymore. I shoved my knees up and almost knocked him over, but he righted himself and leaned into my face again.

I relaxed and cried, "What makes you think you're any better than my father?! You're no better than anyone who has ever hurt me! I can't even get up and go to the bathroom! You're screaming in my face and scaring me. How does that make *you* feel?! Does that make you feel like a man? You are just like the rest. How does that make *you* feel?" Patrick slumped forward for a moment and breathed on my face. I said again, "How does that make *you* feel?"

Patrick sat up and looked at me. I held his stare. He suddenly relaxed, and I pushed him off me. He helped me up but still stayed between the stairs and me. I picked up a T-shirt from the floor, buried my face in it, and cried.

"Can I go to the bathroom?" I asked, blowing my nose.

"No. I'm not through with you yet."

I couldn't run past him, so I ran into my bedroom, picked up the windup clock, and sailed it at him. "I'm through with you!" I cried. I threw shoes, a box of tissues, books, and a framed picture of my father at him. Patrick moved out of the line of fire. When I started throwing clothes hangers in rapid-fire, he ducked into Jason's bedroom. As soon as he was all the way into the room, I ran—down the hall, down the steps, and out the front door. Patrick was right behind me. He went to my car, assuming I would try to reach it, but I was too afraid to attempt the car. I ran.

I ran through the neighbor's yard and down the street. I was barefoot, and the street tore the bottoms of my feet, but I ran on. At first, Patrick was behind me, but after two blocks, he stopped. I decided to run down to the gas station eight blocks away and call Ann to come and get me. I was almost there when I heard Patrick's car. His car muffler had a hole in it and made a distinct sound, so I knew it was him. I hid behind a parked car. Seeing me, Patrick pulled his car to the side of the road and got out. I ran again. I ran through someone's backyard, climbed over a wooden fence, and stumbled right into the unlocked back door of a dark house. I called out but no one came. I crouched down beside the stove in the kitchen and hoped Patrick wouldn't think to look inside. I also hoped no one would shoot me for trespassing. I was a mess. I had on rumpled jeans and a T-shirt, my hair flew wildly around my face, and my toes were bleeding. I put my head on my knees and prayed. *Please, God, don't let him find me.* I could hear him calling. He was getting closer.

"Barbara! Barbara! Come on out, now. I don't have time to play this game with you! Do you hear me? I don't have time to play games. All right, I'm leaving! Do you hear me? I'm leaving and I'm not coming back." He walked by the house where I was hiding, but didn't think to look for me inside. A few minutes later, I heard his car moving on down the road.

My stomach hurt so badly I couldn't stand up. I crouched in the kitchen for fifteen minutes or more, catching my breath and trying to control the shakes. No one found me there. Before I left, I took a paper towel, wiped the blood from the linoleum, and stuffed it into my pocket.

Too afraid to go home, I walked back to the gas station and called Ann. She picked me up a few minutes later.

When I climbed into the cab of her pickup, she said, "What in the world?" She looked me up and down. "Oh, my God, look at your feet!" I started to cry again.

We drove around and I told her everything that had happened.

"You have got to get rid of this guy!" Ann said.

"I need to find him."

Ann slammed on the brakes and we pitched forward. "Are you crazy? Find him for what?"

I burst into tears again. "He's totally lost his mind," I cried. "I just need to know where he is."

Ann threw the truck into park and wrapped her arms around me. "It's all right," she said, patting my back. "We'll find him."

We found Patrick's car parked in front of his Uncle Ray's house, and Patrick standing in the yard with his uncle passing a football back and forth. He didn't look the least bit upset. Ann turned the corner before they noticed us.

"Well, now you know he's just fine," she said bitterly. "I wish I could say the same for you, honey."

Tears rolled down my cheeks.

"Come on," Ann said. "Let's get you home and cleaned up."

Ann drove me home and stayed while I took a bath. Afterward, I pulled on some pajamas and then Ann led me back into the bathroom to bandage my shredded toes. I watched as she tenderly cleaned the cuts. I couldn't feel a thing.

"Maybe I need a gun," I whispered.

Ann looked up at me and frowned. "You *do not* need a gun."

I had had a gun for a while. An old .22 pistol. But shortly after Patrick moved in with me, Ann convinced me to give it to her for safe-keeping. I should have known she wouldn't give it back to me. Instead, she'd dragged me off to a number of demonstrations for women's rights and gun control. And I was glad I went. I'd never really thought about women having rights until I met Ann. And guns—well, I was from the South. I'd never looked at our sorry gun laws. Ann was appalled. "Do you know that three thousand Americans died from handguns last year?" she said. "And in all of Europe only two hundred and forty died! We need better gun control!"

I knew she didn't intend to give back my pistol as long as Patrick was in my life—or maybe ever.

Ann stood up and put her hands on her hips. "You're going home with me."

But I couldn't go. I wanted to be home in case Patrick called. And I wanted to be there when Jason got home so that I wouldn't have to explain what had happened.

Terrified that Patrick would come back during the night, I made a makeshift alarm system by stacking empty cans against the front door. I put Jason's baseball bat next to the rocking chair and tried to sleep.

Several times I thought I heard Patrick shuffle among the sunflowers at the back window, and my heart leapt to my throat. Each time I stilled the rocking chair and gripped the bat, but nobody was there.

The morning light dissipated my fear of Patrick and replaced it with desperation to see him. I thought that if I could talk to him for a few minutes, I'd stop shaking. When I was a kid and my dad would come home drunk and yell at Mother and smash the dishes, I'd be afraid of him until the next morning after he'd slept off the anger and was calm again. Sometimes, if he'd been particularly awful the night before and hurt someone, he'd be sheepish and good-humored until he won us back with pet names and teasing. I was sure it would be that way with Patrick. He'd be remorseful and eager to win me back.

I drove by Ray's house, but Patrick wasn't there. Desperate, I went home and waited. Jason stayed home from basketball practice that evening. I hadn't told him much about what had happened, but Patrick was gone. I'm sure it was obvious that something was amiss.

Two days later, my girlfriend Melanie told me Patrick was staying with Roger, a mutual friend who was also an artist. I called that evening, but he wouldn't talk to me.

"You're scared of me, remember?" he said, and hung up.

I called again. "Patrick, please talk to me. Come over here, or meet me somewhere."

"Not now. I'm having fun. Go take an aspirin and watch TV."

He hung up again. I slammed down the receiver. Exhausted from fear and lack of sleep, I cried myself to sleep beside the phone.

Ann advised, "Forget about him. Please, Barbara, date somebody else." But there was nobody else. There was no me. I had seeped into Patrick. If he wasn't there, I didn't exist. Without him, the nothingness that was my life became vast and dark and terrifying. How long would I be able to outrun it? Just the thought of looking at myself, my own pain, kept me frantic for Patrick's return.

Several days after hanging up on me, Patrick moved into an apartment almost two miles from my house. I knew how far away it was because I drove by every day. Sometimes twice. Sometimes four or five times. Occasionally I'd stop by to see him, and eventually I convinced him to give our relationship another chance. When he finally agreed to try again, I burst into tears and cried, "I'm worth it."

Iitany

*P*atrick pledged his undying love, then took the money we had been saving (quarter by quarter) to go to the Grand Canyon—and caught a flight to California to visit an old girlfriend.

In an absolute panic, I did what my dad had always done when overwhelmed: I smashed the dishes. Pulled every glittering plate, bowl, and cup from the cabinet, marched it out the front door, and smashed it on the front walk. I didn't say anything out loud, but inside I screamed, *You broke this set anyway! What good is a set of china that's missing one plate? Let's just break the rest! Make it a full set of broken dishes. Why have one broken dish when they can all be broken? I don't need a fucking set of china anyway! I don't need dishes at all!*

I destroyed dish after dish and the hysteria ascended. Even though it was freezing outside, and I wore only a sweater, perspiration rolled down my arms and between my breasts. As I stumbled out the door with the last batch of china teacups, a small boy I had never seen before stood over the pile of broken dishes, shivering. He wasn't wearing a coat either and he held his arms stiffly by his sides. He looked up at me with eyes that reflected a familiar terror—the terror I had seen in my brothers' and sisters' eyes when Dad smashed our dishes. The same terror that they must have seen in my eyes. The little boy stood, paralyzed, staring at me. I stared back, openmouthed, as if I'd been caught doing something against the law. Immediately I wondered how long he had been watching me and was thankful that at least I hadn't been screaming out loud. The little boy shivered.

"It's all right," I said, easing the stack of teacups onto the dirty snow. Feeling faint, I sat down on the concrete porch and took a long breath. "It's all right," I said again, trying to smile. "It's just that I don't like these dishes anymore. And I got some new ones . . ." I dropped my head to my chest, breathing heavily, and tried again. "Actually, I'm making a piece of art out of broken dishes," I lied, reaching over and picking up two jagged pieces of a plate and placing them on the porch like puzzle pieces. "See, you take the broken pieces and glue them down on a board in a design. Then you fill in around the pieces with grout—it's kind of like Silly Putty—and you let it dry. You can make all kinds of designs. . . ."

The boy nodded his head as if he understood.

"You need a coat," I said, pushing myself up from the cold concrete. I ran inside and pulled two of Jason's hooded sweatshirts from the hook. I helped the little boy into one and rolled up the huge sleeves, then pulled the other over my head, talking as I went. "I'm using these dishes because they're so pretty. I love the gold edges. It's gonna look really cool." I rubbed the little boy's back to warm him up a little and put him at ease. He couldn't have been more than six years old. I looked around, expecting his mother to come for him any second.

"Where do you live?" I asked.

He bobbed his head to the right. "I'm staying with my grandma. She's sleeping in front of the TV." He looked at the pile of dishes again and his jaw trembled. "I saw you."

"Oh. Well . . . You can help me with my art project if you want to." I reached back into the pile, fished out several glass chunks, and began arranging them into the shape of a tree. "Don't touch the pieces, though. They're sharp. You can break the cups for me if you want to." The little boy's mouth fell open as he stared at the perfect gold-trimmed cups.

"What's your name?" I asked as I added more pieces to the tree. My hands shook wildly and I rubbed them together, pretending that I was just cold.

"Jeremy," he said without taking his eyes from the china cups. "You sure it's okay to break these dishes?"

"Oh, yeah. Several of them were already broken," I lied. "These aren't the dishes I use; I just got them to make art with." I picked up a teacup. "You want to try it?"

Jeremy pushed his hands from the sweatshirt sleeves and took the cup. He looked at me, then looked suspiciously at the sidewalk. He cocked his head to the side and rolled his eyes over at me again.

"It's okay. You don't have to throw it very hard; just toss it over there," I said, pointing down the sidewalk. Jeremy sailed the cup into the air and it landed three squares down the sidewalk and broke into several pieces. He shouted gleefully, then immediately looked around, expecting punishment. I laughed, picked up a cup and tossed it over by the one Jeremy had thrown. It popped like a firecracker, and the handle flipped into the snow. Jeremy laughed, then trembled. I could tell it disturbed him to break the cups, even though I had fooled him with the idea of making art from the pieces. Two cups remained in the snow.

"It's freezing out here," I said. "How about we take these two cups inside and make some hot chocolate." Jeremy stopped shaking for a second as he thought about it, then he nodded and shivered again. He picked up the cups by their fragile handles and handed them to me.

We sat at the table and sipped hot chocolate, both of us shaky from adrenaline and the cold. Neither of us spoke until we had almost finished our cocoa. When Jeremy's cup was just about empty, he held it up to the light and examined it. "These cups look like good art already," he said. "You know, with the flowers and gold and everything."

I held mine up and looked at it too. "Yeah, they do."

"They're the shiniest cups I've ever seen," Jeremy added.

"Yeah, me too."

After we finished our hot chocolate, I rinsed out the shiny, gold-trimmed teacups and gave them to the little boy. I walked him home and thanked him for helping me with my project. For months afterward, whenever I saw children playing in our neighborhood, I looked to see if one of them was Jeremy. But I never saw him again.

come forth

On his way to work one cold, rainy November day, Stewart scraped the side of his car against a tree in his yard and knocked the driver's side door off. He decided he could weld it back on at work, so he tied the door in place with a length of rope and headed for the Anniston Army Depot. A block from the depot gate, Stewart had a seizure, flailing against the door until it fell off again. The car swerved off the road, and Stewart tumbled onto the gravel shoulder and rolled into a drainage ditch. His car then smashed into a telephone pole and caught fire.

The city police just happened to be at the filling station down the street. They heard the crash when the accident happened and drove over to investigate.

"Are you all right?" they said, jumping from the patrol car.

Stewart, soaking wet and covered with mud, crawled from the ditch. "Hell, no, I'm not all right." He fell onto the stubby, brown grass alongside the road. He rolled onto his back and moaned. A huge knot was rising on his forehead and blood was soaking his left pant leg. His teeth chattered.

"I'm freezing," he said, wrapping his arms over his chest and sticking his hands under his armpits.

One of the policemen went back to the patrol car and called an ambulance. The other one got a heavy wool blanket from the trunk, shook it out, and spread it over Stewart.

The shock of the seizure and the icy water made Stewart shake convulsively, and he pulled the wool blanket over his head.

Meanwhile, depot employees drove toward the entrance gate, inching their way along, taking in the blazing car and the covered body on the ground. Someone called Alice and David, who also worked at the depot, and told them Stewart was dead.

"I seen the body laying on the side of the road."

The word spread through the depot like wildfire. Someone called Doris Ann at the YMCA and told her Stewart was dead. Doris Ann called Alice, and the three of them decided to meet at Doris Ann's house.

On their way out of the depot gate, Alice and David passed Stewart's charred car. The ambulance had already taken Stewart to the hospital. The police had waited until the car burned itself out, marked the area with orange cones, and left.

The three of them gathered together, shocked and tearful, paralyzed with grief. But they decided they had a responsibility to go and identify the body, to keep Mother from having to do it.

At the hospital, the emergency room attendant directed them to the fifth floor, where they found Stewart sitting up in bed with a bandaged leg and an ice bag on his head.

Doris Ann stopped in the doorway and screamed.

Alice pushed past her and shouted, "You're supposed to be dead!"

David nudged between them and walked up to the bed. He buried his face in his hands. "Oh, goddamn. You scared the hell out of me."

Stewart lifted the ice bag away from his head. "What in the world is the matter with you?"

Alice crossed the room. "We thought you were dead!" she shouted.

Stewart put the ice bag back on his forehead and pointed to his cut blue jeans. "Look what they did to my blue jeans. The nurse cut them to bandage my leg."

Alice put her hands on her hips. "What?"

"My jeans. They're ruined."

Alice's jaw dropped. Doris Ann came and stood beside her. "We thought you were dead!" she cried, wiping tears from her eyes.

Stewart looked at her and blinked.

Alice grabbed Doris Ann's arm. "Let's go," she said, pulling her toward the door. "Let's go before I kill him myself."

Stewart was completely unaware of the commotion he'd caused. He looked at David. "What's the matter with them?"

David patted Stewart's shoulder. "Don't worry about it, buddy. I gotta get back to work, but I'll be back this evening."

By the time Alice and David made it back to the depot, the word had spread that Stewart wasn't dead after all. Like the man Jesus called from the tomb, Stewart had risen from the dead.

"How's Lazarus?" a coworker piped, and the fighting commenced.

descent

A few days later, on my way to work in the art office, I ran my car into a snowbank. I wasn't hurt, but I couldn't get the car out of the snow. I walked to the art building, but instead of going into the art office, I wandered around in the hall, unsure of where I was. Nothing looked familiar. Filled with panic, I stumbled into the dean's office. His secretary, Jean, a gray-haired woman in her fifties, asked me if I needed help.

"Yes," I said. But my heart pounded in my ears and I couldn't make out what she said next. I covered my ears. Tears trickled down my cheeks. Jean guided me into the dean's office and eased me into a chair. The dean wasn't there. She shut the door and leaned against it. "What is it?" she asked.

"I want to leave this place."

"You want to leave the university?" She sat next to me.

"No," I cried. "I want to leave this planet. I want out of here."

"Oh, Barbara. You don't mean that."

Then the tears came in great sobs. I couldn't stop, couldn't speak. I buried my face in my hands and wailed. Jean reached across the dean's desk, pulled several tissues from the box, and handed them to me. Then she pulled the phone over, sat it in her lap, and dialed. She talked for several minutes but I couldn't hear because I was crying so hard. I suspected that she had called the counseling department, but I didn't care. I wasn't going to a counselor. I'd been to counselors before and knew there was nothing anyone could do for the pain that

I felt. Nothing but Patrick could take this pain away. It was endless. I wanted to go home, but knew I'd have to quit crying in order to get away from Jean. I smiled a fake smile and held my breath so I could stop crying. "I'm all right," I said. But when Jean hung up the phone, she reached over and locked her hand on my wrist.

"You're going over to the counseling office," she said sternly. "I've talked to a friend of mine over there and she's expecting you." I nodded, but was already planning to run as soon as she let go of me. Jean grabbed several more tissues and pulled me out of the chair.

"Come on," she demanded. I caught my breath and tried to force the tears away. If I could dry the tears, Jean would let me go, I reasoned, patting my eyes with my free hand as she pulled me out of the office and down the hall. I stood up straighter and pretended to get control of myself.

"I know where the counseling office is," I said, smiling and tugging at my wrist. Jean clenched my wrist tighter, hastened her step, and didn't say another word. She literally dragged me all the way across campus—in the snow and without her coat—to the counseling office and hand-delivered me to her friend. I collapsed into an overstuffed chair in the woman's office and began to wail. As soon as Jean left, I planned to make up some lie and get out the door. She and the counselor spoke briefly, then Jean turned to me.

"Barbara, this is Liz Wolfsthal," Jean said as she opened the door to leave. "You can talk to her. She's really good. She'll understand."

I nodded, but knew it was a lie. Nobody could understand this pain. I owned it and even I couldn't understand it. How could anyone, especially a normal person, understand anything! And this Liz! She was beautiful, and—judging by the way she dressed—well-off. She couldn't possibly understand anything about the mess I was in. I slumped in the chair and cried even harder. I didn't look to see what Liz was doing; I didn't care. I didn't care about anything except finding a way to hide from the next wave of pain.

Liz waited for several minutes, then attempted to talk to me. "Tell me what's causing you such pain."

When I finally spoke, I screamed and shook my fist. "I want to hurt him! I want to hurt him the way he has hurt me! I want to get a stick and beat him until he bleeds!" I collapsed into sobbing. "Oh, I just want to die!" I cried.

Liz waited until the wailing eased, then leaned forward and took my hands in hers. "Maybe it's just time for the love to die . . . rather than you . . . maybe it's time to let it go."

"I can't!" I sobbed, dropping my forehead onto our clasped hands and rocking back and forth. "I can't."

Liz leaned forward, put her cheek on the back of my head, and rocked back and forth with me, humming softly as I cried.

Fear sent me back to my second counseling appointment. Fear that I might actually die from this heartache, either by accident or on purpose. I was embarrassed that my life was so completely out of my control. I didn't understand how I had gotten into such a hopeless situation. On my own, I couldn't see a way out.

For the next few sessions Liz tried to convince me that I didn't understand the difference between someone who is mentally ill and someone who is trying to avoid emotional pain.

"You think it's different because Patrick is ill—and, yes, he is mentally ill. But you're not schizophrenic, *he* is. You're using Patrick to keep from facing yourself."

I wanted to go home. Liz didn't understand anything. She was from the other side. I stared at the floor.

Liz pulled her shawl tighter around her shoulders and stared at me. "You are creating chaos to avoid emotional pain. When your mind is overloaded, it finds a way to avoid it. But it's time for you to stop avoiding it; it's time for you to get in touch with your soul. Your soul wants a real relationship with you. With *you*. Until you have that, you're not going to be happy."

Offended, I said, "I have a relationship with my soul."

"Do you? You go to school all day, work all evening, keep up with Jason—and all the while you're suffering from a relationship that's not working." She sighed. "Another abusive relationship. Barbara, how many people know what's going on with you?"

I thought about my mother. She knew some of it. My girlfriends,

Ann and Melanie, knew even more. But nobody really knew how dark the sky had become in my world.

Liz sent me home with several books written by women therapists, guides for people like me, who needed to start over but didn't know how. I read them over and over. When the author talked about women who confused pain and pleasure, she meant me. *Me.* The books said that for some women, what was supposed to feel bad began to feel good—especially for those who grew up around alcoholism. So as adults, these women became addicted to the familiarity of an unrewarding relationship. I understood that this described what had been happening to me, but I remained incapable of doing anything about it. I wanted Patrick. I wanted him desperately.

A few weeks later, Patrick was picked up in California and brought back to the psych ward in Des Moines. I visited as much as possible, but it was awful. He tormented me with his interest in other women who were right there in the psych ward: Lily, a pale, beautifully weeping teenager; then Stella, a recovering drug addict in her early forties who had been locked up for trying to burn down the house with her family asleep inside. Stella spent hours every evening brushing and braiding Patrick's hair. To have a conversation with him, I had to sit on the floor directly in front of him because he wasn't allowed to turn his head while she worked. It was ridiculous that I sat there and watched, yet I couldn't seem to make myself leave.

spiral

"Nothing has changed!" I cried to my counselor. "I'm right back where I started, and I think I'm going to die!"

"You are not right back where you were, Barbara," Liz said. "You've made incredible progress since I first saw you. You're addressing the problem, not running away from it. Think of it as a spiral. You climb up, loop after loop, and when you fall—you only fall as far as the bottom of that loop. Not all the way back down." She paused for a minute, then asked, "Are you still reading the books I gave you?"

I nodded. One of them, *Women Who Love Too Much*, had been extremely helpful. I recognized myself on every page. Years earlier, a friend had given me that same book. I'd opened it while sitting in the Atlanta airport waiting for a flight. By the end of the first chapter I was sweating, shaking, and my heart was pounding in my chest. Somehow, the author knew all of the sick and twisted ways I was ruining my life. For a moment I thought I was having a heart attack. I looked around to see if anyone had noticed the sweat trickling down my forehead. As soon as I could get up, I closed the book and stuffed it in the nearest trash can.

Liz had given it to me again. Since then, I'd read it through a dozen times and read parts of it every night before falling asleep. But I couldn't seem to detach as the book advised. Truthfully, I was still convinced that if I just had the right formula, I could make my relationship with Patrick work.

"Tell me about your father," Liz said. "What was he like?"

I thought, *What does my dad have to do with any of this?*

I'd often told stories about Dad to entertain friends, so at first the stories I told Liz were the well-rehearsed ones, the ones that made everyone laugh. She listened and even laughed at some of them, but she pressed for other events in my childhood, the ones that I hadn't created a punch line for. I was reluctant to talk about those days. They made my stomach hurt.

"How much did your father drink?" she asked. "On a weekly basis, how much?"

"He'd get drunk every weekend. Every Friday night, and sober up just in time to go to work on Monday."

"And what was the weekend like?"

"Hell. We never knew what he would do. Smash the dishes, play poker with us, shoot the dog. Every Monday morning, as far back as I can remember, I'd ride the bus to school feeling shell-shocked."

"I think you're suffering from post-traumatic stress syndrome."

"What's that?"

"It's when you constantly *relive* the traumatic events of your life and overwork your adrenal glands."

"So," I said, "it would be better if I didn't remember my childhood?"

"No, *remembering* your childhood and *reliving* it are two different things. Just remembering something doesn't cause your adrenal gland to kick in; reliving it does."

On the way home from my counseling appointment, I decided to forget my past, forget my childhood. I planned to erase all the chaos and start again.

But that night, I woke up at 3 A.M. That wasn't unusual. I woke up every night at that time and would spend the rest of the night mulling over things that happened years ago. On this particular night, I was fixated on 1972, the night my dad was beaten half to death by two derelicts who worked for my uncle. They'd all been drinking together. Somehow the evening went wrong. They beat Dad with a pipe, then threw him into a septic tank and left him for dead. Miraculously, he crawled to a neighbor's house. They brought him home, dragging his unconscious body into the living room. Blood poured onto the floor. And it was that blood—steaming red pools of it—that I couldn't get out of my mind. I'd made a dozen paintings of it: alizarin, cadmium red, scarlet—hot to the touch. But the images were too ambiguous. That night, I got up and sat at the kitchen table, writing as fast as possible everything that had happened that dark night in 1972. The sun came up, and I was still writing.

Several nights later, I decided to put pieces of cardboard and sharpened pencils on my nightstand so I wouldn't have to get out of bed to write down what was bothering me. I woke up, jotted something down, and went back to sleep. The same thing happened the next night, and the next. I knew all these stories by heart, but somehow, writing them down gave them validity—and I could get back to sleep.

Then one morning, I woke up and the cardboard pieces were scattered on the floor by my bed. And I hadn't remembered writing during the night. I picked up the pieces and shuffled through them. I'd written about a time when Dad had disappeared for a while, leaving Mother with seven children. When she ran completely out of food, she washed and cooked poison-coated garden seeds. She ate them, then waited to see if she got sick before feeding them to us kids.

I'd always been able to remember what happened when we were little. But the details in the writing went beyond memory. It felt like I'd gone back to that time while sleeping. A shiver ran through me. Mother wouldn't like this story. She wouldn't like that I'd remembered it, or that I'd written it down. I put the cardboard pieces in a shoe box and slipped it under my bed.

My counselor thought all this purging was healthy. She flipped through my stack of cardboard litanies. "You're finally letting it go," she said.

But I felt like I was coming unglued. I was scared to death of the barrage of images that filled my mind.

Liz held up a piece of cardboard and began reading the story I'd written about my mother. I fidgeted. It felt like betrayal.

When she finished, she looked at me and said, "Go see your mother. Ask her about her life with your father. Tell her what you're going through with Patrick." She waved the card at me. "She's obviously been there."

I crossed my arms over my aching stomach. Liz might as well have asked me to jump out of a plane without a parachute. My mother didn't talk about relationships—and certainly not about her relationship with my dad. Still, I didn't have much choice. My stomach hurt, my head hurt, my hands trembled. I couldn't sleep, couldn't eat. And even a grown woman—when she's hurting—wants her mother.

the faintest breath

My mother lived in a little, run-down house that sat at the edge of the woods overlooking a small valley. You could stand on the porch and watch it rain a mile away. And that's how she had lived her life: watching from a distance. She could withstand anything, it seemed, by removing herself emotionally at the first crack of thunder. Reading books helped her to escape into another world.

One summer I stayed with her for two weeks and we didn't do anything except read one book after another and try to teach her parrot to speak. The parrot, named Shakespeare, had been given to her for her birthday years earlier. All of us kids had pooled our money, then tried to come up with an original idea for a gift. What do you buy someone who needs everything? A parrot, of course. Shakespeare's home, a huge, dome-shaped wire cage from the secondhand shop, was immaculate. Willie had pulled the dents out of it and spray-painted it white. It sat majestically in front of the living room window so that he could converse with the backyard birds.

Through the years, Mother had taught Shakespeare to say "Star light, star bright." That summer, she decided we should teach him the rest of the poem: *First star I see tonight. Wish I may, Wish I might, Hope I have my wish tonight.* I thought that was a tall order for a small green bird, but Mother was crazy about that bird, and confident in his ability to learn. Whenever we walked by, we'd peer inside and chant the poem, hoping he'd repeat it back to us. The front door was wide open and so were the windows. I don't know if Mother had taken off the screens to repair them or if she'd taken them off and thrown them away. That day she was sitting in the rocking chair reading a romance novel, and I was on the couch, flipping through an art book. Shakespeare sat on his perch, cracking seeds and occasionally squawking, "Star light."

Suddenly, Mother's ancient calico cat, Miss Cakes, came running through the open door at full speed, chased by a snarling black cat. Miss Cakes jumped onto the back of the couch, onto the birdcage, down onto the windowsill, and leapt out the back window. The black cat followed right behind her. As soon as they were out of sight, Shakespeare fell from his perch like a dropped rock. Mother and I lowered our books and stared in disbelief at the bird. When it was obvious that he was dead, Mother lowered her gaze to the floor. She was silent for a few seconds. Then, barely audible, she said, "Well, damn," then raised her book and went back to reading.

She reacted similarly when Dad came home drunk one evening and decided to clean out a nest of snakes in the corner of Willie's bedroom. He caught them, all right, and was bitten about fifteen times. Luckily, they were plain ol' black snakes. Mother painted his hands with Mercurochrome and went back to her book. It took a real tragedy, like the time Dad got beaten half to death, to really get her attention.

ᛘ

If past traumas were any indication, this visit wasn't going to be easy. I was sick and exhausted and knew that my life was in danger. I needed my mother to talk to me.

I waited until the morning after I arrived to bring up what was going on. Mother had made grits and eggs for breakfast and gotten out her special blue china teacups just for me. I hated to put a damper on the morning, but I wanted to talk while we had the chance, before Jason got out of bed or someone else showed up.

Mother knew a little about what had been going on with Patrick, but not all of it. Now I told her as much as I dared reveal, and I told her about my counseling sessions with Liz.

"She gave me this book," I said, handing Mother my copy of

Women Who Love Too Much. She looked at the cover and handed it back, but her face didn't harden as I'd expected, and she didn't get up from the kitchen table and start washing the breakfast dishes—a predictable diversion of hers.

"This book is about me, Mom. Almost everything in it—all the crazy things these women do—I've done. I'm still doing them. I can't seem to stop, even though I know it's killing me."

Mother took a sip of her tea. "You think you love too much?"

"Let me read you this list." I opened the book. "These are characteristics of women who love too much." I glanced at the page. The first three items of the list addressed dysfunctional parents and lack of nurturing as the reason women learn this addictive behavior. I didn't want Mother to think I was blaming her, so I skipped them and began with the fourth.

"'Number four. Terrified of abandonment, you will do anything to keep a relationship from dissolving. Number five. Almost nothing is too much trouble, takes too much time, or is too expensive if it will *help* the man you are involved with. Number six. Accustomed to lack of love in personal relationships, you are willing to wait, hope, and try harder to please. Number seven. You are willing to take far more than fifty percent of the responsibility, guilt, and blame in any relationship. Number eight. You are addicted to men and to emotional pain.'"

Number eight was really number eleven, but the hurt look on Mother's face forced me to jump to the one I thought the most important before she stopped me. She took the book out of my hand, and I expected her to close it. Instead, she scanned the pages, then silently read from the beginning all fifteen characteristics. She put the book facedown on the table.

"That's me," she said. "That's exactly how I was with your father." She stared into her teacup and faded into her own thoughts.

I could hardly believe what I'd heard. With all the prodding I'd done through the years, Mother had never talked openly with me. My eyes flooded, but I saw the pain I had caused her and pretended to drink my tea, giving us both time to recover. Mother's eyes filled with tears, and I guessed that she was going over all the ways in which she had cheated herself by staying with Dad. He had abused her physically and verbally for most of their married life—to the point where she didn't react to anything, not even when he abused her children. For most of my teenage years, Mother had been numb. One of the walking dead.

After a few minutes she placed the cup on the table and tapped the book with her finger. "I knew there was something wrong with me. I just didn't know what it was. That's the reason I refused to date after your father left. Even though I had opportunities, I was afraid I'd pick another man just like him."

She sat up a little straighter and tilted her chin toward her chest, a technique for sustaining air supply in the lungs. I'd seen her posture herself that way many times, usually just before she began to sing a song that required tremendous range. To me, even when she wasn't singing, her classically trained voice with its faint, rhythmic Southern accent sounded like music.

"You know, I didn't have anybody to teach me how to be a grown woman," she said. "My mother died when I was a baby, and my daddy raised four girls by himself. He didn't know how to talk to us about men. He didn't know how to talk to us about anything, really. But he tried. He was a good man." She took a sip of tea and cleared her throat. "You think you can control Patrick by how much you love him. You think you can control him just like I thought I could control your father. But, honey, Patrick's sick and you can't change that by throwing your own life away." She paused for a moment and watched me sink into myself. She reached over and rested her fingers on my wrist.

"I didn't know alcoholism was a disease until it was too late. I thought it was me; I thought your father drank because of me. But he was sick. He was sick—and Patrick is sick, and you can't change that." She stood up and started gathering the breakfast dishes. "When you get to feeling better, I want you to go home, and I want you to stop this nonsense. Read that book and figure out what to do. Take it step by step and day by day and keep doing it." She put the dishes in the sink and looked at me. "I don't want to lose a daughter over this mess; and I don't want you to be an old lady like me, living all alone and lonesome. I want you to go out there and find a man that's not crazy or drunk or both."

I fought back tears again. "That's what I'm trying to tell you, Mom. I can't do it. I've tried. But all I can think about is Patrick. If he'd just take his medicine, everything would be all right. He goes into the hospital and they get him on it, but as soon as he walks out the door, he quits taking it. I've done everything I know how to do—"

Mother interrupted. "He's not going to take his medicine. Just like your father couldn't stop drinking. And even though you and Patrick both know he's got a disease, if he won't take care of it, there's nothing you can do. It's time for you to stop thinking about Patrick and start thinking about yourself."

I dropped my hands in my lap. "I can't."

"What about Jason? Do you want him to wind up without a mother?"

I shook my head, and tears ran down my face. Mother studied the floor at her feet for a minute, then walked over and pulled open a drawer and came back with a wide rubber band.

"Stick out your hand," she demanded. I stuck out my hand, conscious of how badly it shook. She stretched the rubber band and snapped it onto my wrist.

I jerked my hand away. "Ouch."

"There." She walked back to the kitchen sink. "Now, every time you think about Patrick, snap your wrist with that rubber band. Eventually your mind will refuse to think about him at all."

I wiped my nose on the back of my hand. The rubber band tumbled down my arm like the faintest breath on my skin.

"That's aversion therapy," Mother said as she squirted dishwashing liquid into the sink and watched bubbles rise. "You see, surprised as you may be, I know a thing or two about psychology."

a little respect and love

When I returned from visiting my mother, Liz said, "ACOA meetings. Adult Children of Alcoholics. I think it could do you a lot of good."

Insulted, I said, "But I don't drink."

"ACOA is for the *children* of alcoholics, Barbara. That's you. In fact, you have all of the manifestations of the disease—you just don't drink. Think of yourself as a dry drunk."

"That's ridiculous," I said.

"You need a support group. You're going to graduate in a few weeks, and I want to know that you'll be okay." She stared out the window for a moment. "Promise you'll go. At least for six weeks. Promise me."

I nodded.

ACOA meetings were held at the Presbyterian Church on Saturday mornings. About twenty people, men and women, all ages, sitting around a long wooden table. On my first visit, I went stone-faced and unapproachable. I thought, *I'm not one of them.* Someone started the meeting by reading the twelve steps for codependents. The steps were just a revised version of the Alcoholics Anonymous twelve steps. I thought ACOA was like preaching to the choir. Then the meeting was turned over to whoever needed to talk. I wasn't about to talk in front of these people. I didn't know them and they didn't know me.

And I didn't believe for a minute that listening to their sad stories could help me. *I* wasn't sick. Patrick was sick. I was just trying to help him.

The first person stood up to speak. She talked, but made no sense.

"I'm Cheryl."

"Hi, Cheryl."

"I'm worried. The thing I'm worried about . . . Well, I worry all the time, and I know that's something the program can help me with. That feeling like, worrying about what's gonna happen, not in a realistic way but in sort of an unrealistic way. I know it's from growing up. It's affecting how I'm looking at my life now, and it's not a positive thing. I just feel like I've got all this stuff hanging over me, this idea that we're not in control of our destiny, our lives. I don't know." Pause. "It's good to be here. I'll pass."

She sat down, and I almost bolted for the door. I imagined reporting the meeting to Liz. *I didn't get anything from that meeting! They made no sense! How can I learn anything if they don't make sense?*

Still, I started going to as many ACOA meetings as possible, simply because I didn't know what else to do, where else to look for comfort. I sat through each meeting without speaking a word.

The year before, while I was in Alabama, I had gone to an AA meeting with Stewart. The group consisted of eight men and (not counting me) one woman. Everybody smoked and everybody drank cup after cup of hot, sweet coffee. I couldn't wait to get out of there. But even now, I could still remember something one man said. He was referring to the physiological aspects of alcoholism. "My brain doesn't work right," he said. He pointed to several people, including my brother. "And neither does yours." Everybody nodded in agreement. The man took a sip of his coffee, then added, "It takes a long time of being sober before your brain gets balanced out."

As I sat through the meetings for Adult Children of Alcoholics, I began to ponder what that old recovering alcoholic had said. My brother Stewart was trying to stay sober long enough to regain the balance in his brain. Yet, I didn't drink, and my brain didn't work any better than his. It was a scary thought. Crazy with alcohol, crazy without it.

❧

One Saturday morning I was only half listening as different people spoke of their concerns and disappointments. Then a beautiful thirty-year-old woman told my story as clearly as if I'd told it myself. She didn't speak loudly, but you could have heard a pin drop in that room. It seemed that all the women were glued to her words.

"I pick the same unavailable man every time," she said. "I beat myself to death trying to save some guy who isn't the least bit interested in saving himself—and he's not the least bit interested in me either, but I can't stop. It's like a drug. This guy I'm seeing—I spend half my time talking to him on the phone explaining the last conversation I had with him, explaining how I felt. I pour my heart out. Then at night, we fight about what was said over the phone. He tells me I'm too needy. And it makes me unsure of myself. Am I too needy? Am I asking too much? All I want is just a little respect and love. When I talk to him about what I need—which is for him to cut back on his drinking and spend some time with me—he shouts 'Too needy!' like I'm asking for the moon. He doesn't help with the bills. I've caught him with several women, and he says it's my fault. He said if I knew how to keep a man happy . . . I'm so afraid he'll leave me that I'll do anything. My bank account is empty. He says he's moving out. Last night I tried to get him to talk to me, but he didn't say a word. I asked him why, and he said I talked enough for both of us. He says I talk too much, weigh too much, want too much. With everything I do for him, he acts like it's all he can do to tolerate my presence. I'm so upset I can hardly think. I feel like I'm going crazy, like I'm going to die."

Halfway through her story I started to cry uncontrollably. Someone pushed a box of tissues in front of me, and I wailed. I was still crying when the meeting was over. As I was going out the door, an older gentleman grabbed my arm and shook it. He said, "Recovery sure looks good on you." I shook my head and kept moving toward the door. I didn't feel like I was recovering. I felt like I was dying.

revelation

On a warm June day, in the midst of a psychotic episode, Patrick jumped off the roof of the Artists Building. He landed on a large, trampoline-like canvas sculpture that was attached to the first floor. It broke his fall, but he was still pretty battered. He'd jumped during a big art opening with lots of guests, and it caused quite an uproar. Alarmed by the police cars and news of the jump, the guests left, ending the art opening before it really got started. The Artists Building manager gave Patrick sixty days to pack up his art supplies and get out of the building.

After he'd been released from the psych ward, Patrick came by the studio, and while he boxed up supplies and stacked them by his table, he smoked and watched me work. He dropped his cigarette and ground it onto the floor with the toe of his black wing tip.

I hated for Patrick to smoke and he knew it. I hated it worse when he smoked in the studio because the expensive rag papers I used absorbed the smoke. But he was angry with me and I wasn't about to mention smoking. He pulled out a pack of cigarettes, tapped it against his finger, and shook one out. He adjusted the cigarette in the corner of his mouth, lit it, and caught it between his fingers. He came over and stood beside me.

"Are we going to get back together or not?" he asked, blowing smoke into my face. "I know you're going out with that doctor. I followed you. Now I want to know if you're going to stop." He put the cigarette back in his mouth and stalked across the room to get something to use as an ashtray. The tone in his voice made the hair on my arms stand up. While he had his back to me, I hid my utility knife under a box of charcoal.

"Stop working and get over here!" he yelled. I wiped my hands on a rag and walked over.

"Well?" he said, pinching out the cigarette and dropping it into a tin can. "Are we going to work things out, or not?" He put the can on the floor and nudged it out of the way with his foot.

"Patrick, I don't think we can get back together. I can't take another chance on our relationship. I've started over and over with you, but we can't make it work."

Patrick closed the distance between us in two steps. He leaned forward until he was within an inch of my face. His eyes were clear and sharp and angry. "I want you to stop seeing that guy," he whispered. "Are you going to stop?"

Patrick was right. I had been out with someone. And he was kind and interesting and, more than anything else, attentive. He *wanted* to spend time with me.

"No," I whispered, "I'm not going to stop seeing him. It's a chance for something real—"

Patrick grabbed me by the shoulders and shook me. "What are you talking about, you silly bitch?" He threw me against the partition that divided the studio, pulled me toward him, and slammed me into it again. The wall cracked and collapsed backward to the floor, taking me with it. Patrick pulled me up by my collar and shook me until my teeth rattled. "What are you talking about?" He grabbed my wrists, squeezed them together, and dragged me over to his worktable. He threw me onto the table and began slapping me in the face, screaming, "You are such a silly bitch."

As soon as Patrick began to hit me, it felt as if my soul left my body. I knew he was hitting me but I couldn't feel it. As I was thrown onto the worktable, I heard pencils and pens clatter to the floor. I heard the birds squawking outside the studio window and one of my hoop earrings fall onto the concrete floor and roll away. I tried to pull away, but my arms wouldn't do what I commanded. It felt as if I were somewhere else altogether.

I thought about my mother. She had been too afraid to break away from my dad—afraid that he would hurt her, afraid that he would hurt himself. "It's not his fault," she'd say. "It's the drinking. He'll be all right in the morning." I had done the same thing for Patrick, blaming his behavior on schizophrenia. But just as I knew the stagger and slur of alcoholism, I knew the stilted movements, the altered reality, and hollow-eyed look of schizophrenia. Patrick had just gotten out of the psych ward; he was on medication; he wasn't psychotic now. He was hitting me and knew exactly what he was doing.

I curled inward, the blows sounding like a ball hitting soft, weathered wood, and an incident from my childhood came to mind. Dad was yelling at Mother. She stood perfectly still, silent. I was standing in the doorway, ready to run if necessary. The fight transfixed me. Dad reared back as if to strike Mother, but she didn't try to protect herself or fight back. As if I were the one about to be struck, I lifted my arms over my head to block the impact of the blow. Dad saw me and staggered a little. I dropped my arms and fled. But not before shouting, "Kick him, Mom! Kick him!"

I snapped back into my body with a shout.

"This is why, Patrick!" I screamed. I bit him on the arm but he didn't let go of me. "This is why! This is the reason I can't get back together with you! This is not the way you treat someone you love!" I twisted around and kicked him in the chest as hard as I could. He fell backward, wrenching my wrists and pulling me off the table. My knees dug into his side as I collapsed on top of him. He dropped his hold on me and groaned. For a second we breathed, too numb to move.

"This is why, Patrick," I whispered, and began to cry. Blood dripped from my mouth onto his neck. Patrick wrapped his arms around me and began sobbing. I buried my face in his neck; tears collected in the hollow of his throat. "I can't do this anymore; I don't want to be afraid of the man I love." Patrick squeezed me tighter and cried out loud. The sound of his weeping penetrated my bones. I closed my eyes and cried with him.

When our tears subsided, Patrick sat up and pulled me to him. He reached over and took a clean paint rag from a box of supplies and wiped my face, then my hands. He rubbed my wrists with his palm. Pain shot through my arm. I cried out and held it against my rib cage.

Patrick wiped his nose on his sleeve and struggled to get up. "I'd better get you to a doctor," he said. He lifted me to my feet and ran his fingers over my wet eyes. "I'm so sorry, Barbara. This is not what I'm really like, not what I wanted for you."

I nodded and wiped tears from my chin. "I know."

Patrick brushed off my clothes and wrapped my coat around my shoulders. He put his arm around me, and we walked slowly through the studio building to the parking lot. My car was parked next to his. We leaned against my car, tears streaming down our faces. Patrick took my keys, unlocked my car, and opened the driver's side door.

"Your mouth is bleeding," he said, wiping my lip and running his hand down my arm. "Let me take you to the doctor. I think your arm might be broken."

I shook my head. "It's not broken. I just want to go home."

"I really think you need a doctor. I'll tell them what happened."

I burst into tears again and shook my head. "If I need to go to the doctor later, I'll let you know. Right now, I just want to go home." As I eased onto the seat, I groaned with pain. Patrick cried out, then squatted and lifted my legs into the car. He put his forehead on my thigh and cried.

"Please, don't hate me, Barbara."

I ran my hand through his hair. "I won't."

"Promise you won't hate me."

"I promise."

That night I dreamed my dad was chasing me. I was about seven years old and we lived in a house with no inside doors. You could run through the house in a big circle, ending up where you started. In the dream the house was dark and sinister, but the furniture—obstacles in the path of my running—fascinated me. I hadn't seen most of it since I was a girl. In the middle of the kitchen floor sat an old Formica table with the aluminum trim sticking out from one rounded corner like a snake about to strike. Gushing smoke and flames leapt from the living room sofa. Mother's rocking chair, empty and broken, rocked fiercely. On the bed lay old familiar toys: a metal cash register, a Slinky pull toy, clamp-on roller skates, empty paint-by-number boxes.

I ran past these things with the overwhelming desire to touch them, but not daring to stop for fear of being caught. Dad chased me from the kitchen, through the bedroom, and into the living room. I quickly outdistanced him. But when I ran into the next room, my dad changed into Patrick, and Patrick chased me the rest of the way, gaining on me with each step. I ran on, with the pursuer changing from Patrick to Dad and back to Patrick. I awakened from the dream with a start, trembling and drenched in sweat.

destiny

When I was a kid, the city of Birmingham decided to reroute Village Creek so they could build a freeway. They moved the water—changed the direction it ran. But every time it rained, really rained, and the creek was under stress, it went right back to its old channel. I had been like that creek—changing, only to slip back to familiar behaviors under stress. But after Patrick hit me, I couldn't go back. The love was still there, the pain of living without him was still there, but my heart had been broken so completely that there was no picking up the pieces.

Edward, the doctor I had begun seeing, ended our relationship because I wouldn't turn Patrick in to the police. That evening, he had driven me to his office to take an X-ray of my arm. He examined the bruises on my face and begged me to press charges.

"He's psychotic, Barbara," he said. "He's dangerous. You don't have to be afraid of him. The police will protect you."

Obviously his experiences with the police had been different from mine. And besides, I wasn't afraid of Patrick, and I didn't want to turn him in to the police. I didn't believe for a minute that he'd intentionally cause me more pain—and I also didn't believe that he had been psychotic when he hit me. Deep down in my sick heart, I was glad that losing me had meant enough to make him violent. It was one of the few times that I really believed he had loved me at all.

Even with a bruised face, I longed to see Patrick. I didn't know how to *exist* without him. Didn't know how to cook dinner, read a book, or make art without feeling as if I would go out of my mind. I didn't know what I needed or how to get it. I felt like a newborn baby that needed a slap on the back to jump-start breathing. And like a newborn, I wanted my mother. Hoping that just being in her presence would help me find my way, I flew home again.

When she picked me up at the airport in Birmingham, she hugged me, then held me out and looked at me from head to toe as if checking to make sure I was still in one piece. "You're not going to see him anymore, are you?" she asked.

I shook my head.

"Good. Now you can move on."

I nodded in agreement, but truly, I had no idea what that meant, or how to go about it.

The next day Mother and I drove out to visit my brother Stewart. He was sitting on his front porch drinking Jack Daniel's straight from the bottle. When he saw us, he started to cry and climbed from the steps and stood in the doorway as if to block us from entering his home.

"It's terrible inside, Mom," he said.

Mother hugged him and said, "I didn't come to see your house. I came to see you."

It hadn't been long since I'd seen Stewart's house. He had never taken good care of it, but this time it was in shambles. It was as if the sky had fallen. We walked through the house to the living room, sunlight pouring through the windows, and I could see dust drifting in the air, settling on tattered spiderwebs that clung like giant bats in the corners of the room. On the bookshelf, dusty, framed pictures sat untouched for so long the faces were unrecognizable. Mother and I sat down on the couch, and the stale smell of whiskey shot through my head. Stewart sat in an old, overstuffed chair, shaking miserably.

I watched him take a sip of whiskey and thought about the difference drinking had made in his life. He didn't read the newspaper anymore, didn't pick the guitar anymore, didn't jog or swim, joke or play.

The three of us sat talking about the weather, then covered all that was going on with the family, but we didn't talk about what was happening in our own lives: his addiction, my addiction. I was only half listening to the conversation anyway. The wind whistling through the boards at my feet and the cracked windowpanes threatened to steal my breath. Whiskey—the very smell of poverty. I closed my eyes against the fear and felt twelve years old again—the trace of whiskey coming from my dad, and the loose floorboards from any number of long-ago houses we'd lived in. I sucked in a sharp breath and counted the minutes until I could get out the door.

By the time we got up to leave, my heart was skipping beats.

Later, Mother and I sat at her kitchen table, drinking hot tea. She said, "It's killing him." She meant alcohol. But then, rather aimlessly, she added, "I ought to burn that house down. Maybe then he could get a hold on his life."

I was astonished at the boldness of her statement, and to hear her invoke fire as a second chance. When we were kids, living in a house where the fireplace was the only source of heat, my mother seemed fixated on fire and its dangers. Fire was a thing to fear, both in shortage and excess.

Mother took the two boxes of matches from the mantel and dropped them into her dress pocket. "What do you do if the house catches fire while I'm gone?" she asked.

Alice groaned. "I already told you."

"Well, tell me again."

"I grab John from the crib and run outside. Stewart grabs Doris Ann. David and Barbara and Willie run out the door." Alice pointed out the window. "We all go to that tree over there and wait for you to come back. We don't try to save our toys. None of them."

"That's right," Mother said, looking at each of us. "Don't stop for anything. Make sure everybody is safe. And don't go back inside—no matter what. Is that clear?"

In unison: "Yes, ma'am."

Doris Ann toddled over and sat down on a log by the fireplace and rocked it back and forth. Mother went over and scooped her up. "Let's not play with that, honey." She put her in a chair at the kitchen table. "All of you come away from that fire. Come over here and sit at the table until I get back."

"But it's cold," I said, sliding into the chair beside Doris Ann.

"I know it's cold," Mother said, guiding Willie into a chair. He sat at the head of the table where Dad usually sat, and David stood beside him.

"I can put that log on the fire," Stewart said.

"No," Mother said. "That's the last one. We'll wait a bit." She sighed. "I want you kids to sit here and draw. Make me a picture to hang in the living room. Alice and Stewart will help you." She opened a kitchen cabinet and got out several yellow pencils, a small box of crayons, and some notebook paper and put them on the table. Then she went to the closet and pulled out a long, camel-colored coat. She held it by the fur collar and shook it as if checking its weight.

Mother had had that coat as long as I could remember. In the summer, she'd wrap it in paper and put it in a trunk to keep the moths from eating it. In the winter she'd get it out and wear it, and sometimes, when it got really cold, she'd put it on our bed as an extra blanket. I loved to snuggle my face into the fox-fur collar and let it tickle my eyelids as I rocked myself to sleep.

Mother pulled the coat over her housedress and buttoned the top button, took a black scarf from the pocket, flipped it over her head, and tied it under her chin. My heart raced every time I saw her in that coat. She looked so different—so beautiful—as if she didn't belong to us at all. I beamed with pride, and she smiled at me.

"Alice," she said, "don't let any of them go near that fireplace."

Alice said, "Yes, ma'am."

Doris Ann slid from her chair and toddled back to the log. Alice grabbed her by the arm and she struggled to get free, fussing. Mother picked her up and moved her away from the fire once more. Then she picked up the cold log and sat it near the table.

"Here, baby," she said. "You can sit on it now." Doris Ann sat on her log and rocked happily back and forth.

Mother walked back to the fireplace and stared into the low flames. Then she took Dad's crowbar from the closet and walked out onto the back porch. Us kids ran to the window, pressing our faces against the frosted glass just in time to see her slide the crowbar under the window screen and pop it loose. She dropped the crowbar on the porch and brought the screen inside.

"Now," she said, standing the screen in front of the fire and propping it up with red bricks, "that makes it a little bit safer." The frost that had formed on the screen melted and a thin trickle of water ran across the hearth. Mother watched it evaporate, then herded us all back to the table.

As she finished buttoning her coat, she walked to the crib and looked down at John, her seventh child. She tucked the blanket snugly around him and kissed his cheek.

"I'll be back as soon as I can," she said. "And, Stewart, don't feed that fire. I'll be back before it goes out."

"Mom," Stewart said, "I'm eight. I should go with you." He straightened his shoulders and stood on his tiptoes.

Mother ran her fingers through his tight, dark curls. "I know, honey, but I need you to help Alice with the babies. Can you do that for me?"

Stewart nodded, disappointed.

Mother opened the door and the wind blew our drawing paper off the table. Once outside, she cupped her hands to her eyes and peered back in through the window just as we scrambled for the flying notebook paper. I looked up and saw her frowning face.

"We're not supposed to be out of our seats," I cried, climbing back onto my chair. Then the wooden boards creaked as Mother stepped off the porch and onto the frozen ground, and we all ran to the window. We watched as Mother put the ax in the wheelbarrow and pushed it in the direction Dad usually headed when he went to chop wood. When she got to the birches that lined the edge of the forest, she looked back to check on us, and we jumped away from the window.

"Did she see us?" David whispered.

"Of course she saw us," Stewart said. We waited then, eyeing each other, allowing Mother plenty of time to move on down the dark path into the woods, then Stewart sneaked back to the window.

"Is she gone?" Alice asked.

"No," Stewart said. "She's just standing by the trees. Maybe she's waiting for Dad."

"He won't be home till it's dark," Alice said.

"Maybe she's afraid of bears," I said.

Stewart laughed. "She's not afraid of bears."

Annoyed, Alice said, "Is she still standing there?"

Stewart peeked again. "Yep." He looked over his shoulder and said, "She's afraid we'll burn the house down."

Alice peered through the icy glass and nodded in agreement. Little by little the rest of us made our way back to the window. Mother blew on her hands, her warm breath escaping like smoke between her fingers. She stood staring back at the house, the wind flying her scarf out behind her like a flag. Then, after several minutes went by, she walked to the porch and picked up the crowbar she'd dropped there after prying off the window screen. Suddenly she slipped the thin, curved end between two porch boards and snapped one loose.

Alice huffed. "Mrs. Johnson is sure going to be mad." Mrs. Johnson owned our house. The last time she'd come to collect rent, she had pointed and complained, "Who on earth drew on the walls? What happened to this window? Where is my flower box?"

We had all drawn on the wall: it was smooth and white and big enough for making houses and trees. Willie had cracked the window tossing his toy trumpet at David for cupping his hands together and bellowing like a moose, and Stewart was using the shallow, dirt-filled flower box as a home for his snapping turtle.

Mother dropped the crowbar and lifted the end of the board. It popped like a firecracker. She twisted it back and forth, wrenching it from the grip of the nails at the other end, then pulled on it with all her might. It came loose with a snap. Mother stumbled backward off the low porch with the long board in her arms, and swung in a circle in the yard as if dancing, a look of surprise on her face.

Inside, we all gasped and looked at each other, our eyes and mouths wide as saucers. Willie started to cough. Alice pursed her lips together. Stewart said, "Ha." I cupped my hands and peered again through the window.

Mother grabbed on to the post that held up the porch roof and leaned against it to steady herself and catch her breath. Then she stood the board on its end. It towered over her head. She looked at it as if she wasn't quite sure what to do with it now that it was free. I know she saw us, out of the corner of her eye, but she didn't glance our way. She dropped the board against the porch, pulled the wheelbarrow closer, then lifted the ax overhead and gave the board a fierce whack. It cracked in two and fell to the ground.

"Oh, my stars," Alice said.

Mother picked up one of the pieces, leaned it against the porch again, and chopped it in half. *Whack. Whack. Whack.* She tossed the cut pieces into the wheelbarrow and splinters jumped from the bed like summer grasshoppers. She blew on her hands again, rubbed them together vigorously, then picked up the crowbar and snapped another board from the porch. She ripped it free just like the last one, dragged it to the edge of the porch, and dropped it.

"There's my red car," Willie shouted, pointing at the gap where the board had been.

"And the spoons to my tea set," I cried. Mom and Dad had given me the tea set for my fifth birthday. Dad had gone to get it early that birthday morning, and I had sat on the porch waiting until he returned that evening, only to immediately lose the tiny spoons through the cracks.

"Mom!" we shouted. "Mom!"

She heard our commotion but still didn't look our way. She reached into the hole and collected the plastic car and spoons, slid them into her coat pocket, and set back to work. *Whack.* And the board splintered. *Whack,* and it fell to the ground. Willie and Doris Ann covered their ears. Baby John woke up and started to cry, and Alice went to the crib and brought him back, blanket and all, propped on her hip. She tapped on the window. "There's Mommy," she said, scooting him higher on her hip. "There's Mommy." John sucked in his breath, turning this way and that, looking to see what was causing the racket. Alice nudged us aside and tapped on the glass to get Mother's attention. John slapped it with his open hand, gurgling. Mother lifted the ax over her head, slammed the wood, and it cracked like thunder, rattling the windowpanes.

Resolved now, Mother slowed her pace and chopped with a steady rhythm. And when she dropped the ax to stack the wood, she began to sing: "The last time I saw Paris. Her trees were dressed for spring, and lovers walked beneath those trees, and birds found songs to sing."

Stewart looked at Alice. "Do you think she'll chop down the whole porch?"

Alice hiked the baby on her hip. "Mrs. Johnson's going to pitch a fit anyway. She might as well chop down the whole thing."

And she did. One board at a time until the porch frame stuck out of the hard, red earth like the rib bones of a huge fish.

When she was done, she brought in an armload and stoked the coals of the dwindling fire. The old, dry porch boards flared, shooting sparks toward the window screen, and the room warmed. Mother took the baby in her arms, kicked off her shoes, and wiggled her cold, red toes while we got close to the hot flames and dug into her coat pockets for our toys. She kissed John on the head and sang, "The last time I saw Paris, her heart was warm and gay. No matter how they change her, I'll remember her that way."

That night, I couldn't sleep. Mother's comment about torching Stewart's house stuck in my head and played over and over.

The next day I borrowed her car, supposedly to visit a friend, and drove out to Stewart's to burn his house down. It's a thirty-minute drive through pastures and pine forests. Alabama the beautiful. But I wasn't looking for beauty—I was looking for redemption. Maybe starting all over would make things work for him, I thought. And if he could do it, then maybe the rest of us could—maybe I could.

I pulled into Stewart's yard, turned off the engine, and rolled down the windows. No one was home. I didn't expect anyone to be there. It was quiet except for the tapping of some rusty wind chimes hanging from the back porch. I got out of the car and stood with the matches in my fist. Sunlight danced through the cracked window-panes in the kitchen. Even though the back door was open, I didn't go inside. I was afraid to be in there without another living soul to shield me from the suffocating deprivation that permeated the place.

Trash littered the yard and the wind blew a weathered scrap of paper against my shoe. Without moving closer, I tried to see through the windows, tried to recall what was in each room, what treasures would go up in smoke.

"You did this, Dad," I whispered. "It's your fault. All of it."

I kicked at the ground and thought about the drawings Stewart used to make: sailboats. Sailboats with full billowing sails, heading for the deep blue sea. I thought about how much he must have wanted to sail away from all the problems that showed so hauntingly through those windows. But he hadn't sailed away. He had stayed.

Dad had stayed too. It's what I admired most about him, actually. The idea of leaving, abandoning us completely, surely entered his mind. Drinking must have called to him and begged him to abandon ship. Between his dire circumstances and the demands of a wife and eight kids, anywhere but home would have been less stressful. But he didn't leave. Not for very long anyway.

Still, even though I loved him and I was glad he didn't go, it occurred to me that we might have been better off if he had. Maybe Stewart wouldn't have followed him down that same path to destruction. Maybe I wouldn't have.

I thought about the generations of men on my dad's side of the family. *How far back would I need to go before I found the right person to slap silly?*

Eventually I sat down on Stewart's back porch. Its boards were beginning to rot from age and from the old newspapers and trash bags heaped all over it. One board was broken and a small piece of it stuck out like a loose tooth. I snapped it off and peeked through the crack, finding several colorful beer-bottle caps nestled in the red dirt. I tossed the board to the ground. Stewart's porch would burn hot and fast like that old porch Mother had chopped for firewood.

I gathered up a pile of newspaper and cardboard, lit a scrap of paper, and let it burn down to my fingers, then dropped it into the pile. I jumped off the porch and watched as it leapt into flames. But before the fire caught the boards, I jumped back onto the porch and kicked the flames out into the yard.

I couldn't burn down Stewart's house. I couldn't hurt him any more than he had already been hurt. And even in its present state, I didn't know what the house meant to him. I tossed the matches into the dirt and drove back to Mother's house.

I looked over Jordan
an' what did I see

Stewart got sober. He told me how it happened. He told me a dozen times. He'd call me up on the phone and start at the beginning and tell the whole story, in full detail, as if he hadn't told me before. The details never changed. I believe it happened just as he said.

Stewart pulled a half-empty quart of Jack Daniel's whiskey from the refrigerator, walked across the kitchen, and set it by the sink. He licked his parched lips and tried to twist the cap, but he was shaking violently. He put the bottle on the counter and ran his hands over the seat of his jeans as if warming himself. Tears welled in his eyes; he dug his fingers into them. "God help me," he whispered as he picked up the bottle again.

"I sent Kenneth," someone said from the living room. Stewart put down the bottle and looked behind him. Anyone could have been there. He'd drunk half the whiskey the night before, but he could still remember Kenneth stopping by. Yes, Deuce had been there too, and Coon Dog.

Deuce had been sprawled on the couch when Kenneth walked into the living room. Deuce snarled at him, "Not the fuckin' Bible-thumper."

Now morning light beamed through the window above the sink.

Stewart winced, propped his elbows on the counter, and dropped his face into his hands, waiting for whoever was there to come to him. When no one came, he walked toward the living room, holding his head with both hands. He eased his shoulder against the door frame and peered into the room. "Who's there?" he asked, and waited. He pushed away from the door frame and made his way back to the kitchen.

Saliva welled in his mouth. Leaning forward, he spit into the sink, straightened, and picked up the whiskey bottle. This time he wrenched the cap off and it fell, rolling against a bag of trash that had spilled onto the floor. Sweat beaded on his forehead. He lifted the bottle.

"I sent Kenneth," someone said.

Stewart spun around and called out, "Who's there?" He put the bottle down. "Deuce?" he said as he went back to the living room. "Coon Dog?" He walked to the couch and snatched up an old army blanket. "I'm too sick for this shit today, Deuce!" He put one knee on the couch seat, leaned over, and looked behind it, then glanced behind the overstuffed chair and the battered TV set.

"I sent Kenneth," someone said. This time Stewart thought the voice came from the bedroom, or possibly the kitchen. Trembling, he dropped the blanket to the floor. "Kenneth?" he called out. "Kenneth?"

Stewart didn't want to see Kenneth. Kenneth had crossed over a line that Stewart couldn't find. Astonished—and jealous—he'd watched it happen. Somehow, Kenneth got sober. But with his sobriety came this unbelievable sanctimonious bullshit that was infuriating.

"If I can quit, you can quit," Kenneth had said. "Come to the meetings with me. Come to church. You can quit." Every time Kenneth came by, he'd preach that shit. He wouldn't let it go. But Stewart knew that *he* couldn't quit. He'd been trying for years. He'd been to the evening AA meetings at the high school; he'd been to the morning ones at the Moose Lodge; he'd even tried the noon meetings at the military depot where he worked. On more than one occasion, he'd been drinking. Once, at a meeting at the lodge—he'd drunk two beers beforehand to ease his nerves—he'd told them to kiss his ass, called them all a bunch of fakers.

Stewart inched toward the bedroom. The hardwood floor was

uneven and splintery under his bare feet. He thought of pummeling Deuce and Coon Dog. It had to be one of them. One time they caught a raccoon in a burlap bag and tossed it through his bedroom window at three in the morning. The pissed-off raccoon destroyed half the bedroom before scrambling back out the window. Scared the hell out of him. Kenneth had been in on that too.

The door to the bedroom was partially open. Stewart eased it the rest of the way and looked around. It had been two years since the raccoon had been in there, but the room was still a mess. Most of the clutter had been pushed against the wall. Stewart didn't clean. He washed dishes, clothes, and sheets. Everything else stayed dirty. Occasionally, he'd sweep, but only enough to clear a path from room to room. The house was basically the same as it was the day his wife left.

She'd left him years ago. Stewart thought he'd surely die. But he had insisted on keeping the kids with him. Helen and Kevin. They were little then. He'd had to keep living—or at least go through the motions. As the years passed, the kids got older, but his life remained the same. And so did the house. Only a lot dirtier. Giant cobwebs hung from ceiling to bookcase to dresser.

Stewart looked behind the door. "Coon Dog?" He looked at the unmade bed and considered climbing back into it, but as much as he needed to lie down, he needed a drink more. Tremors swept through him and he reached out to steady himself—laid his palm down on a pile of AA tokens on the nightstand. He lifted it and two tokens stuck to his damp hand; they didn't fall, even as he brought it close enough to read them. TO THINE OWN SELF BE TRUE, 24 HOURS. UNITY, SERVICE, RECOVERY, 3 MONTHS. That was the longest he'd ever made it.

Without whiskey, there was nothing between him and the world. These people he couldn't talk to. This sober world that rushed in like a dragon. Every hour of sobriety made his heart pound like a jackhammer. Every day he thought of dying.

Trying to get sober had helped him understand his dad's death. One bullet to the head. He'd been diagnosed with cancer and couldn't drink anymore. But it hadn't been the cancer or the chemotherapy or the pain that was killing him. It had been sobriety. He couldn't stand his own presence.

There were endless reasons to quit drinking. His body stayed in a constant state of shock; Helen and Kevin wouldn't let him see his grandbabies when he was drinking; his job was in jeopardy. But the look on his mother's face was what haunted him. That staunchly optimistic gleam he saw in her eyes. He could feel it on him even when she wasn't there. It broke his heart. She was so sure he would beat this thing. He hated that hope she held. She'd never taken a drink in her life. What did she know about it?

Walking back through the house he called out, "Go home. Go home, Kenneth!" but when he reached the kitchen, no one was there. He looked around the room, then quickly turned in a circle, glancing through the house again. The hair on his neck stood up. A fierce shiver swept through him. He shouted, "Kenneth!" and immediately felt faint. Tears welled in his eyes again. *Was he going crazy?* No, it was the whiskey. He'd had plenty the night before and hadn't had much sleep. What he needed desperately was the hair-of-the-dog. He stumbled to the sink and grabbed the bottle.

Trembling, almost giddy, he lifted the whiskey. Just as the cool glass touched his lower lip, a force pulled it away from his mouth and suspended it in midair. Stewart strained his arm against the force and tried to put his mouth to the opening, quivering as the bottle balanced just out of reach. The cool morning air changed to a hot mist, and sunlight blazed through the window and door, filling the room with an undulating hum. Stewart struggled frantically to win the bottle. Adrenaline surged through him and he felt charged with strength. With murderous rage he wrenched his arm.

"By God!" he shouted.

The voice said, "Yes."

Stewart felt something grasp his right arm, and then his left, like a bear hug from behind, the weight of a mountain pressed against his back. With all his strength, he wrestled for the whiskey. Within seconds his energy was spent and he began to falter. He shook convulsively.

"Please!" he shouted. "I have to have it!"

The bottle slowly twisted away from him until the whiskey spilled into the sink, sizzling when it hit the cool basin as if it were hot grease from a frying pan. Stewart choked and tears ran down his face.

"No!" he cried.

"Yes," the voice said.

Exhausted, Stewart released the bottle and it smashed in the sink. Desperate for a drink, he pushed the broken glass aside trying to wipe up the whiskey with his hand. The basin sizzled again and in a blast evaporated the last of it and sent Stewart flying backward. He crashed to the floor, as if he'd been struck by lightning. Vivid colors flashed behind his eyelids. Then flickering images: collecting eggs from the henhouse with his mother—her soft coo to the chickens; washing dishes in the big aluminum pan and handing them to his sister Alice. A storm. Working on a car with his dad and his brother David. His dad saying, "Hold it steady."

"Stewart?" his mother called.

"Stewart?"

Then he saw his brothers and sisters. Grown. Looking much like the last time he had seen them. They were standing by his casket. Photographs lay on the breast of his favorite shirt. His sisters were crying.

Then he was above the casket, examining the body. There was something about it. His hair was the same—hands, chest. A few pounds thinner, but that wasn't it. It was as if he hadn't died but had merely been taken—eased into the hereafter.

Stewart opened his eyes and squinted into the sunlight that poured through the kitchen window. He sat up, scooted against the wall, and began to cry. Great gasping sobs. Tears different from any he'd ever known before. Good, warm, and light as air. At first, he couldn't remember why he was crying. But then it came to him: the formidable light. Searching his memory, he covered his eyes with both hands and held his breath, afraid that even the act of breathing would erase what he was trying to recall. The image drifted in and out and in again. He had seen his funeral. The casket—the body! He had seen his face, chest, the weight of his dead arms, the curve of his dead fingers. He began to laugh and cry at the same time. His body in the casket had been thinner, but beyond that, it had been at ease. Untroubled. He had been sober. Long sober.

troubling deaf heaven

Years earlier, when Stewart had helped me move to Iowa, he told me what it felt like to quit drinking. He said his heart and mind raced, he shook uncontrollably; he didn't know what to do with his hands and panicked when forced to make conversation.

"My sponsor says that will all go away eventually," he said. "If you can make it through withdrawal, you've got a good chance of survival."

And he meant *survival*. Addiction was killing him. And it was killing me. Living without Patrick—without my addiction—felt exactly like Stewart's description. I couldn't sleep, couldn't eat, couldn't think. My hands shook and my heart fluttered. I was going through withdrawal.

To stay focused, I made a list of everything I wanted to accomplish in the next few years: avoid crazy men, find an art-related job, buy a decent car, help Jason with college.

Sending Jason off to college scared the hell out of me. I hadn't dropped dead from fear and exhaustion, self-pity and grief, because I was needed. I was—above all things—Jason's mother. Sick and shaky, I'd gone to all of his senior basketball games, attended parent/teacher meetings, filled out college applications, and guaranteed student loan forms. Every evening I'd listen to stories about girls and teachers and basketball practice—shots from center court that went right into the hoop—and I'd thank God he had been born. I didn't know exactly how I had pulled it off, but I knew that somehow Jason had made it.

Shortly before his high school graduation, Jason accepted a college basketball scholarship. He was so proud of himself. It had been a dream he'd been almost too afraid to dream, and he couldn't believe it had come true. Unfortunately, it was a bittersweet victory. To accept this scholarship, he'd have to move hours away—hours away from his girlfriend, Amanda. She had another year of high school. Jason would have to go it alone for a year, and he was sick about it.

Through the years, as Jason and Amanda's relationship had grown, I'd watched with quiet fascination. *How in the world had he learned to sustain a long-term relationship with me as a role model?*

"I don't know if I can do it, Mom," Jason said as we packed his clothes. "I've seen Amanda every day since I met her. I don't know if I can make it till Thanksgiving."

I knew exactly how he felt. I'd seen Jason every day since the day he was born. I wasn't sure I could make it to Thanksgiving either.

A few days later we unpacked his clothes in his dorm room. We put up his bulletin board and the posters from his bedroom wall. I filled his car up with gasoline and gave him the last of my cash.

"You're all set," I said. I'd been feigning excitement all day. My face felt frozen from smiling when I really wanted to cry. I hugged him tight, told him I loved him, and left, holding my breath so that I wouldn't break down until I drove out of the parking lot. As I drove back to Des Moines, I shook so badly that it felt as if the car were trembling.

I don't know how I made it back home. As soon as I opened the front door, I was confronted with a brand-new fear, being alone. The broken lock on the window above the kitchen sink had been a comfort should Jason or I need to break into the house, but now it felt like an invitation for burglars. I dropped into the rocking chair and listened. The house made noises that I'd never heard before: creaks and bumps and moans. But familiar sounds like Jason's basketball slapping the wall, the TV and the radio playing at the same time, telephone conversation, and the shower running—the noises of my daily life—had stopped.

I reminded myself that letting go was part of being a good mother, but it didn't help. As long as Jason had been around, I'd had a reason to keep moving, a reason *not* to stick my head in the oven. Without him—well, I wasn't sure of anything. I started to cry, and cried and cried and cried. An hour later I rolled out of the rocking chair onto the living room floor, curled into a ball, and rocked back and forth as I prayed out loud, begging God for comfort.

The phone rang, startling me. I pulled it to the floor and rolled onto my side to answer it. The voice on the other end sounded far away.

"Barbara? Are you there?"

"Yeah."

"Barbara, it's Dawn. Do you remember me?"

I did remember her. At one time, Dawn and I had attended the same church. One Sunday she had given me a ride. On the drive home that day, a car swerved in front of us. She shook her finger in the air and said, "That man is going to hell. He cut me off on purpose and he'll pay for it. God will see to it." I was appalled that Dawn thought of God as her personal hit man. I couldn't wait to get out of her car. I avoided her at church and hadn't heard from her in over a year.

"Yeah," I said again.

"I heard you crying."

"What?"

"I heard you. I was washing dishes, and as clear as a bell, I heard you crying."

I started to cry again. Dawn told me help was on the way. That God wouldn't leave me alone. Everything would be all right. She talked on and on, repeating herself. But it didn't matter what she said. She had heard me crying, and if she had heard me, it was possible that God had heard me too. I pulled myself up, climbed back into the rocking chair, and dried my tears.

Several hours later, Jason drove into the yard and dashed into the living room. He held his chest as if he'd been running. "I can't leave yet," he said. "I'm not ready to leave home yet. I'll go back if you tell me I'm not welcome here. But I want to stay. At least for this semester, I want to stay home and go to community college. If that's all right with you?"

PART 5

Iowa City, Iowa, 1993

the promised land

A year slowly tumbled by. I created a body of artwork inspired by Alabama and continued to write down the stories from my childhood as they came to me. Slowly the pain in my heart melted. I began to feel strong.

Jason moved back home and enrolled in the community college. One day he sat at my computer, writing a paper for his psych class. The assignment was to find a psychological situation in real life, change the names, and analyze it. He was having a difficult time coming up with a case study.

"You can use me," I said. "Since Dad died, I've been pretty crazy."

"Nah," Jason said, "you're not crazy enough."

In a year, I'd gone to ACOA every week and snapped myself silly with that rubber band Mother had put on my wrist. I wrote my favorite quote by Aristotle in huge block letters on my studio wall—*You Are What You Repeatedly Do*—and set about *doing*. I went through the motions every day until I became whom I had wanted to be all along. *A woman, a mother, an artist, a dreamer, a wisher, a hoper, a prayer, a magic bean buyer.*

Since graduating from Drake, I'd been teaching art part-time at the local museum, and working part-time in a dental office. I had also been looking for an art-related job that paid well—a seemingly impossible task—and then, somehow, I found one: director of Discover Art, a state-funded program at the University Hospital in Iowa City. The University Hospital was part of the University of Iowa, the college Jason planned to attend the following year.

"I'll transfer now," Jason said. "If you need for me to go with you."

"No. I'm fine," I said. And it was true.

In Iowa City, I rented a small, white house with hardwood floors and a picture window, just two blocks from the hospital, close enough to walk to work. The last time I had moved, I had spent $150 for a secondhand bedroom set and a tattered couch. Hoping for nicer things in my new life, I left most of the furniture with Jason when I moved. For my Iowa City home, I bought living room furniture from a *Good Housekeeping* magazine prop sale. The brick-colored couch coordinated beautifully with my ocher rocking chair. In the afternoon, sunlight splashed through the picture window and bathed the living room in a soft, warm glow.

And when I wanted to (or had the time), I could make more art. This house had a studio. It was supposed to be a family room, but since I was living alone, I used it as an atelier. Large windows filled two sides of the room, and a tile floor made it easy to clean up paint spills and smudges left by dropped brushes. It was a great place to work. The entire house came together so beautifully that I could hardly believe it was mine.

My childhood traumas continued to wake me at night, but they didn't swallow me up like before. I was still jotting down the stories on cardboard that I kept on my nightstand. The cardboard pieces had grown to the size of shingles, and I had enough of them to roof a house.

Right after I moved to Iowa City, I dreamed my heart was hurting so badly that I pulled it from my chest, held it in my hand, and looked at it. It was made of pale linen. The edges were tattered because a thick green worm had burrowed into the fabric and was slowly eating it. I laid my heart on the counter, picked up a kitchen knife, and began stabbing the worm. The sound was sickening—like the crunch of a catalpa worm when you thread it onto a fishhook. I kept stabbing it. As the body of the worm was reduced to pulp, I vomited. It spilled from my mouth, down my chin, and onto the floor. When the worm was finally dead, I stuck the tip of the knife into its bludgeoned body and pried it from my heart.

When I woke up, my chest was pounding fiercely. I knew the worm was symbolic of pain and loss: all the hurts and disappointments and fears and doing without. It was symbolic of Dad's drinking, the sorrowful fact that his own pain had turned him into a raging alcoholic who would eventually put a gun to his head, and of Mother placing her life on a shelf when she realized she couldn't save him (or herself) from that rage. The worm that had burrowed into my heart felt like all my suffering—and the suffering of past generations. *And the sins of the father shall be visited upon the heads of the children.*

Jason gets angry when I talk about inherited sins. "What kind of God punishes children for the sins of the father?"

But God isn't doing the punishing. The fact is, we lived so close, breathed in our parents' insanity, we became infected. God isn't saying, *I'm going to punish you because your father was a crazy alcoholic who shot himself in the head.* God is saying, *You will suffer because your father was a crazy alcoholic who shot himself in the head.* It's a warning, something to clue you, make you pay attention to your own actions— be aware that you might not be acting in your own best interests, or the best interests of your children.

Falling in love with Patrick had been a way for me to focus on someone, and something else to numb the pain and confusion of losing my dad to suicide. I'd just look away, I told myself. I've since learned that you have to look. Look right at it. Cry. Quake. Scream. Fall on the floor. And that's what I did, eventually. I took the long, painful route, but eventually I staggered into the light again.

grace

After thirteen years of single parenting, I married. Thirteen years after my last divorce, I married a hard-to-find man. He makes coffee, works on Jason's car, makes frames for my artwork. He writes me love letters in disguised handwriting and sends them in unmarked envelopes.

There are days when I long to argue, fight over forgotten phone calls, money that disappears like ice in hot sweet tea, suspicious callers that hang up in the night, the deep disappointment gnawing away at my heart.

But there are no fights, for there are no forgotten phone calls. I gnash my teeth, force myself not to think about the challenge, the familiarity of an unrewarding relationship. Addiction: to excitement. Addiction: to pain.

I do not want it anymore. But it calls my name sometimes in the still of the day, when nothing is moving. Will I be able to resist? Long term, will I? Will I be able to keep that wolf from my door? Breathe slowly: in your nose, out your mouth.

It's all at my fingertips now: love, friendship, stability, even fairness. Sometimes I have to rock my head at night: back and forth, back and forth, blocking the urge to run, run, run, run, run, looking for one more chance to repair the past. I pray, "Please, God, don't let me fall from this sweet grace."

The Jesus Table

*I*nspired by Dad's light-up picture of Leonardo da Vinci's *The Last Supper*, I decided to create a work of art that incorporated that image with other images from my childhood. And I wanted it to be large. My studio was only eleven by eleven feet, so I bought a piece of Masonite panel four by seven feet. My husband, Duane, helped me lay it out on sawhorses so that I could work on it from all sides. The long, narrow board filled the center of the room, leaving just enough space to walk around it. Onto the panel, I sketched *The Last Supper*, all twelve disciples and Jesus sitting around a long table, with my dad added on one end. I painted Jesus' halo yellow and his hands bright red. I drew my sister Alice, at the age of six, sitting in a rocking chair holding a gladiola blossom. Her rocker sat in front of Jesus so that he looked out over her head. Oversize gladiolas shot up from the bottom of the composition—bright red, purple, yellow, and pink, their spiked tops jutting toward the Son. A thin, blue Latin-style cross ran the length of the board, its crossbeams stretching just above the chatting men.

To finish the piece, I intended to pour a thick layer of beeswax over it to soften the images and blend them, then write with oil sticks on the pale wax (after it cooled) a paragraph from my journals. I'd already chosen a paragraph about left-handed people, one that insinuated that Jesus was left-handed too. But by that time, I'd worked so hard on the piece that I chickened out of pouring two gallons of hot wax over it. *What if I ruin it?*

I didn't touch the piece for months and months. In fact, it sat so long it became a table. It was the perfect place to wrap birthday and Christmas presents or put together frames for smaller artworks. If I needed the scissors, I'd more than likely find them on *The Jesus Table*. If my husband, Duane, searched for Scotch tape or a screwdriver, he'd find them there too. *The Jesus Table* became a household word, like *sofa* or *rocking chair;* it had a location and a function.

In the spring, a new gallery opened in Iowa City, and I managed to book an exhibition for fall. I started working on a new body of work for the show: tall gladiolas with bright red blossoms surrounded by indigo sky, a portrait of my mother holding eight baby robins, self-portraits that documented the metamorphosis of my life, dark houses, crooked tornadoes, fire. But *The Jesus Table* lurked in the back of my mind. If I could finish it, it would be perfect for the show. *But what if I ruined it?*

One Saturday, Duane and our friend Rich sat on the front porch drinking beer and talking about Harley-Davidson motorcycles. They'd been out there all morning. I was in my art studio. I'd known for some time that I'd need help to finish *The Jesus Table*. It was really large, and pouring two gallons of hot wax uniformly over it was going to be a real trick, if it could be done at all. My help was lounging on the porch. They didn't balk at the idea. If fact, they were delighted to be a part of it.

My studio had an old stove. As I stirred the pot of melting wax, Duane and Rich stood around *The Jesus Table,* studying it. Duane had seen it many times, but Rich hadn't.

"Do we get to sign our names at the bottom too?" he asked.

I laughed. "Listen, if this actually works, you can sign it anywhere you want."

Rich put his hands on his hips and moved around a sawhorse until he was standing in front of the piece. Suddenly his eyebrows shot up and he leaned over for a closer look. "Is that your dad sitting at the table with the disciples?" He blinked, then straightened. "Oh my God, he's drinking a beer and holding a cigarette." He looked at me, a shocked expression on his face. Then he turned to Duane. "You know we're gonna go to hell if we help her with this, don't you?"

Duane laughed and nodded.

I stirred the wax. "We are not," I protested. "God loves art."

Rich stepped back. "I'm gonna stand over here. Just in case a bolt of lightning comes crashing through the roof."

The plan was for Duane and Rich to hold the long Masonite painting at an angle, and I would quickly pour the hot wax down the surface. I'd been practicing with smaller pieces. It worked best to build a dam of clay around the panel so that the hot wax could be poured uniformly over the surface of the art. Heating the panel in the oven ahead of time helped the wax stay liquid until it reached the desired thickness. But *The Jesus Table* was too big. I couldn't build a dam around it or put it in the oven. My chances of achieving the effect I wanted were minuscule. Still, in my heart, the piece needed a thick layer of pearlescent wax to give it the feeling of passing time. Nothing else would do.

When the pot of wax was ready, Duane and Rich lifted the panel from the sawhorses and held it on either end. I poured the wax. As soon as it made contact with the room-temperature board, it hardened and formed a thick, rippled mess, like stalactites hanging from the ceiling of a cave, and the excess puddled and hardened on the newsprint that covered the studio floor.

"Dammit!" I shouted, pouring the wax faster. "I'm ruining it! I knew it!" I got to the end of the artwork, empty pot in hand, and stared in astonishment. "It's a mess!" I cried.

The guys were stunned into silence. They lifted the panel back onto the sawhorses and stared at it, their mouths slightly ajar. Wax dripped from the sides of the panel, forming columns as it hardened. Duane's brow furrowed and he pinched his upper lip together with his thumb and index finger. I tossed the empty pot onto the floor, gearing up to pitch a big fit.

"The iron!" Duane shouted. He dashed from the studio and came running back with my steam iron. He shook the water out of it and slapped the plug into the wall. "This'll work," he said, licking his fingers and tapping the iron until the moisture sizzled. Duane was an engineer and knew these things.

I grabbed the iron and set to work. The guys went to the kitchen for a beer and came back to watch the show. They leaned against the wall and went right back to their conversation about the virtues of a Fat Boy.

The iron burned hot and melted the wax too quickly. "This is not going to work!" I shouted.

"Turn it down," Rich suggested. I turned it down, and down, and down, until it melted the wax at a slow rate, allowing me to manipulate the wax as the iron slid across the surface. Inch by inch the wax evened out and the image underneath began to take shape. Two hours later *The Jesus Table* had a quarter-inch layer of pearly wax from top to bottom. The disciples and my dad looked old and faded; six-year-old Alice floated in space behind the bright new gladiolas. The willowy blue cross lurked just below the waxy surface like a haint.

I picked up a black oil stick and wrote on the surface, *Mother had once told me that most creative people were left-handed. She meant artists and writers, but I imagined by the way Jesus held his left palm up and his right palm down, that he too was left-handed.*

At the gallery opening in September, a couple in their forties admired *The Jesus Table*. "How long did it take to do this?" the man asked.

I thought about his question. It was one I had been asked many times. *The Jesus Table* had taken a long time, but in reality, no longer than the oil stick drawing of a gladiola that looked like a string of pop beads, a one-minute sketch. It wasn't the amount of time spent on one piece that mattered, it was the accumulation of years—a love affair with the movement of it all. The living line. How could I explain to him that it was a lifeline sent flying into my deepest dreams?

The man looked at me, puzzled. "How long?" he asked again.

"Forty-two years," I answered.

PART 6

Iowa City, Iowa, 1997

wild cat

Over the summer it rained for two weeks. Water flooded the streets. One day, while I stood on the porch watching rain cascade from the roof, I heard a kitten squalling behind our house. I took the umbrella and went around back to see if I could find it. He was hiding in the high weeds. I tried to catch him, but he took off like a shot around the side of the house. I hoped he'd gone home. But in the middle of the night I heard him crying again. The next morning I tried to catch him. After several failed attempts, I talked Duane into helping me.

"If we fence in that back area with something, cardboard or chicken wire, we can trap him back there. Then I'll go in and get him."

"It won't work," Duane said.

I'd been awake all night listening to the kitten yowl. It had taken me back to my childhood, to the nights my dad came home and made my mother cry, or my sister Alice, or me. About the time I would fall asleep, the kitten's wail had snapped me awake and made my heart pound in my chest.

"If you don't want to help me, I'll do it myself," I told Duane.

Reluctantly Duane pulled old boxes from the garage, sliced the sides apart and taped them together to make a fence at each end of the house.

"This isn't going to work," he said again.

"He's just a baby, Duane. If we don't catch him, he's going to die."

"He's wild, Barbara. You can't catch a wild cat with cardboard."

I clenched my teeth. "You just don't want to help me."

"All right. Tell me what you want me to do and I'll do it."

We installed the cardboard and I sneaked into the fenced area and inched toward the cry. Before I got close the kitten streaked past me, climbed right over the cardboard, and fled across the road. I ran after him but lost sight of him behind the neighbor's house. I looked and looked and called and called.

"You can't catch a wild cat that way," Duane said when I arrived back home. I was angry. Duane hadn't wanted to help me in the first place, and now the kitten was gone. Lost in the rain.

"He's going to die out there. Drown or get eaten by an owl."

"He'll be okay," Duane said. He rubbed my back and tried to hug me, but I was too upset to accept comfort. "Listen. I grew up on a farm. We had lots of cats—some of them wild. I know about wild cats. If you want to catch him, feed him. Put food out every day and let him see you and get used to you. Eventually he'll come out."

"That could take forever," I complained.

Late that night the kitten was back behind our house. As soon as I heard the first wail, I put some tuna on a saucer and sneaked out to the weeds. I tapped on the saucer with a spoon and called out, "Here, kitty kitty." But the kitten ran farther into the brush. I stood outside in my nightgown in the dark, calling and tapping for an hour.

"Come to bed," Duane called from the upstairs window.

"Shhh."

The next morning the food was gone, so I filled the saucer again, tapped on it to call the kitten to breakfast, and hid behind the corner of the garage. After a while the kitten sneaked out of the weeds, a black, gleaming-wet fur ball hardly bigger than a mouse. So hungry he shook. He grabbed a bit of food and ran back into the weeds. Cautiously, he sneaked out again, his yellow eyes blazing with hunger, looking everywhere before he scarfed down the tuna. He was much smaller than I had anticipated, too young to be away from his mother. I had to catch him before he drowned in the rain or starved or died of pneumonia or sheer fright.

And so it began. Hour after hour. The next day it stopped raining. I took the welcome mat from the front door out to the weeds and placed it about eight feet from the food dish. I sat on the mat in the warm sun and recited poetry, sang songs, meowed like a mother cat. Morning, noon, and night, singing, "Buffalo gals won't you come out tonight, come out tonight, come out tonight. Buffalo gals won't you come out tonight and dance by the light of the moon."

When I stopped singing, the kitten cried.

"The owl and the pussycat went to sea in a beautiful pea-green boat."

On the fourth day, the kitten came to the edge of the weeds as soon as I tapped on the saucer. When I sat down and began to recite poetry, he came out of hiding. I had been moving the mat closer to the food dish each day. As the kitten began to eat, I reached out to pet him. He fled into the brush and I fell backward, exhausted from it all. Nearly a week had passed. The painting on the easel in my studio hadn't been touched in days, and the kitten was far from tame enough to catch. I was frustrated.

Then suddenly I sat up and stared at the spot where the kitten had disappeared into the weeds. It dawned on me that it had been just like this when I was trying to catch a glimpse of my own soul. For a moment I was stunned, stunned that I had, in fact, accomplished what I had set out to do, which was find myself. I thought about the time I'd invested over the last few years coaxing my soul out of hiding. My soul had been as skittish as this wild, desperate cat.

On the eighth day of singing to the wild cat, he walked up to me and put his nose on my hand. I didn't waste any time; I snatched him up and ran inside. Once inside the house, he hid behind the sink in my art studio and began to cry all over again. It took a week to lure him out, to hold him and pet him and take him to the vet. The veterinarian said he was seven weeks old. That meant that he was five weeks old when I first heard him cry out. Just a babe.

After the kitten got used to me, I named him Einstein, partly after Duane—who looks like a more handsome version of the great physicist—and partly because this kitten was so smart. When he was about three months old, I thought I should have named him after a superhero; that cat could defy gravity. The neighbor's dog chased him across the yard toward the garage, both of them running full speed, the cat spitting and hissing. When Einstein reached the garage, he ran straight up the side without a second's hesitation. The dog ran headfirst into the wall and nearly knocked himself dead.

Einstein is skittish, even now. He's afraid of loud noises, sudden movements, and strangers, yet I've watched him pull snakes right out of their holes, wrestle them lifeless, and fling them around as if he were playing with a rope. I've never seen anything like it. He's a little bitty thing, but he can drag snakes ten times his strength from the weeds.

I can't help but think that I'm a lot like that kitten: still skittish—afraid of the dark, afraid of what I can't see clearly—but brave too. I know now that when I have to, I can stand up to anything that might appear in my future and anything that might slither out of my past. I can fight and win against powers ten times my strength. I know I can. I've done it before.

the pony story

Through the years, I've prided myself on the fact that I remember the events of my childhood. I've considered it a gift—and sometimes a curse. When my brothers and sisters can't remember something about our past, usually something nonsensical that Dad did, they'll call me. I remember these things.

My first memory is of sharing a crib with my brother David. I'm about ten months old; David is almost a year older. He is lying on one end of the crib and I'm on the other. Our feet meet in the middle. David starts kicking his legs in the air as if he's riding a bicycle. I'm watching him, fascinated by what he's doing. Then I kick my leg, realize I can do what he is doing, and joyfully kick into the air. I've been told that I couldn't possibly remember that far back. But I do.

A few days ago my baby sister, Janet, called. We got to talking about Dad and the crazy things he'd do. Janet said that she believed her life changed the day Dad shot her pony.

"I was about four years old," she said. "The blood splattered all over me, and everyone else, and Mom rushed us inside and wiped us down with a wet kitchen towel."

I had heard the pony story many times from other siblings. Each time I heard it, I said, "I wasn't there. That must have happened after I got married." Several years ago I told my brother John that I must have been at work when Dad shot that pony. Whatever the circum-stance, I was certain that I had not been there. And I was thankful not to have been.

I listened to Janet tell the pony story and once again said, "I wasn't there."

She ignored me and went on, "Dad shot him at close range and the blood went everywhere. There wasn't anything wrong with him; Dad was just mad at Mother. We were out of horse feed, so Mother had tied the pony to the fence near the house so he could eat the grass. The fence was barb wire, and he scratched his neck and front legs trying to get to the grass on the other side. The cuts weren't bad. Mother doctored them with iodine. But when Dad saw the pony, its fur all patchy with rusty-colored iodine, he was furious. Of course it was all Mother's fault. To punish her, he shot the pony right in front of her. Right in front of me." Janet paused again, choking back tears.

I choked too and said, "Thank God I missed that one." We fell silent.

The pony story changes with the teller. According to my brothers, he had been tangled in the barb wire and couldn't get free. Dad *had* to shoot him. I didn't know for sure, but I knew that it didn't matter. Either way, Dad shot that horse in front of Janet—and she felt a shift in the course of her life.

Janet began to talk again, continuing her version of that day. She said the explosion of the rifle echoed against the forest and came tum-bling back at them like thunder. She thought for a minute that it was thunder. And then she went beyond the shooting, telling information I'd never heard before. "Dad got Edson Tucker to come over with his tractor and tie a rope on him and drag him away."

Then I saw it, clear as a bell—the tractor dragging the dead pony through the freshly plowed soybean field behind our house. The wet, red mud guttered on either side of the pony like a wake left by a boat. As the image became clearer, the hair on the back of my neck stood up. I closed my eyes and felt the dishcloth Mother was using to mop the pony's blood from my face and neck.

I dropped the phone into my lap, but I could still hear Janet's tear-choked voice. "Edson dug a hole with that ol' backhoe and buried him at the edge of the woods. I could see the grave from the back steps." And then she was silent.

I picked the phone up but couldn't say anything. Then I told her I had to go and hung up. I sat for a long time trying to remember the details of what had happened that day. The images felt just out of reach. I sat perfectly still, straining to hear Mother's voice, the crack of the rifle, but the memory didn't magically materialize. Still, I had been there after all, and the realization of it shot through my bones, and tears poured down my face.

It began to get dark outside and I didn't want to remember what had happened anymore. Most of all, I didn't want to hear the gunshot, and I was afraid that if I went to sleep, it would come back in a dream. Duane stayed up with me most of the night. I rocked in the rocking chair and tried to reason with myself: *How could I be so upset over a pony that died thirty years ago?* Still, the loss weighed heavy in my chest. Night faded into dawn and I didn't remember anything more.

The next morning I called Janet back and told her I had been there, that I remembered Edson pulling the horse away, remembered the blood.

"I knew you were there," Janet said. "I was little, but I knew you were right behind me."

"Why didn't you say something before now?"

"I don't know. I thought maybe it was a good thing you didn't remember it. I sure wish I didn't."

"I still don't remember the actual shooting. I just remember bits and pieces. What bothers me the most is that every time David has said he doesn't remember something happening, I've gotten mad at him. I've always thought he was trying to make out like nothing ever happened. I've never believed him. Now, I don't know what to believe. I was always the one who remembered everything. What if there's more?"

"There's not," Janet said. "One of us would have told it by now."

"Yeah. You're probably right."

Janet and I both sighed, then laughed shakily.

I said, "Sometimes I think he'll never be dead long enough not to hurt me."

"Me too."

"Do you still love him?"

"Yeah," Janet answered.

"Why?"

"I don't know."

"Me neither."

epilogue:
asking a favor

*T*wo years after Stewart got sober, he died of congestive heart failure. At first I was devastated, and so were my siblings. *How could he die?* we wanted to know. *He'd finally stopped drinking whiskey for breakfast, stopped driving drunk.* In the many months of his sobriety, we'd stopped waiting for disastrous news, exhaled all our fears with a deep sigh. Just when we thought he was safe, he died.

It took a while for me to see his death in a different light—one that had more to do with him than me. Months later, it dawned on me that maybe death wasn't such a terrible thing. Here on earth, Stewart had done the hard work—reclaiming his life. Maybe being snatched up like brand-new shoes was his reward. Maybe.

Recently, his daughter, Helen, who is in her twenties, wrote to me, asking a favor.

Dear Aunt Barbara,

I'm sorry I haven't been able to pay you back the loan. I have every intention of paying it back. I hope you believe me. I don't like to ask for help and I hate it more when I can't pay it back. I guess that's Daddy's pride in me.

I do have one more favor to ask of you. In your last book you wrote about Daddy being an alcoholic. If you are going to write about Daddy in your next book, please tell some of the good stuff about him. He was so much more than just an alcoholic. Tell about how Mama left him—and he insisted on keeping us kids. He raised two children, by himself, and he was a great daddy. Even though he drank, he was never abusive and we felt loved. Write about how he stopped drinking—on his own, how he got saved and baptized, and starting playing his guitar for the church service every Sunday, and later became the superintendent of the church.

Aunt Barbara, I don't know if you know all of this, but Daddy was a sponsor in his local Alcoholics Anonymous group. He was a spokesman at the county meetings and helped set up a 1–800 number for counseling alcoholics who couldn't (or wouldn't) come to the meetings. He was also the treasurer for that group.

Speaking as his daughter (who was there), he was not a bad man or a bad father. I love him as much now as when he was alive. Sometimes even more, and occasionally, I think he will walk in the door. I miss him very much. I just don't want people to think my daddy was nothing but a drunk.

Thanks for everything.

Love, Helen

P.S.

I have a few memories that I'd like to know if they are true. When we were little, did Jason and me go on an overnight trip? Did you take me to a Halloween party when I was about eight years old? And did you take me swimming? Janet was there. And Darrell and Chris, and Jason. I remember kicking the water and laughing. Did any of this happen?

Acknowledgments

Without my husband, Duane DeRaad, my friend Kate Kasten, and my friend and editor, Sarah McGrath, my writing would be mere chicken scratch. Thank you so very much. Thank you to my friend Jim Autry, whose guidance and honesty were indispensable.

Thank you to the incredible women at Scribner: Susan Moldow, Nan Graham, and, again, Sarah McGrath. *Y'all* are the greatest!

Thank you to my agent, Wendy Weil. I hope we get to do this many times.

Immense gratitude to Ann Wright Au, Melanie Parks, and Ingrid Mazie for carrying me through the rushes. You know you did.

Thank you to my son, Jason Freeman Moss, for occasionally dragging me out into his sunshine. Thank you to my brothers and sisters, Alice, David, Willie, Doris Ann, John, and Janet, for their love and support—and great tolerance as I've tossed bits of our lives into the sky. (I am you.) Thank you for sharing your memories on these events: Alice for *maverick,* Willie for *magic,* Doris Ann for *making crazy,* John for *come forth* and *Alabama kicking at the moon,* and Janet for *the pony story.* A special thank-you to my brother Stewart for sharing his journey with me, and for giving me permission to write it. May he ride a new Harley in heaven every day. Thank you to Helen Moss for the beautiful letter.

I am also in debt to Michael Carey and Karman Hotchkiss for their work on the early draft of the manuscript. Thank you to my friends Lindsey Henry Moss, Don and Joan Rinner, and Jan Weiss-miller, for reading the working drafts, and for being so enthusiastic about it.

Kathy Albright, Richard Borchard, Diana Cates, Valerie Chittick, Grace Conaway, Claudia Corwin, Adrienne Drapkin, Kathy Gloer, Charlie Langton, Joni Russ, Ann Scholl, Linda St. John, Barb Standish, Shari Stevens, Doug Warner, Rich and Casey Webster, Tom and Kathy Wegman: I am honored to call you *friend.* Thanks for the support and the laughter.

Thank you to Kate Davey, Michele Hostetler, James Howe, Candida Maurer, Nicole Nisly, Brent Overton, Michael Santangelo, and Edward Wallace for putting Humpty-Dumpty back together again.

Thanks to Mom and Dad for teaching me to dance.

And thanks to Daniel—and again, to Daniel.